Turnaround/Restructuring Playbook in the Kingdom of Saudi Arabia and the GCC

Naif Al-Rasheed

Contribution by
Faisal Nawaz

Turnaround/Restructuring Playbook in the Kingdom of Saudi Arabia and the GCC

Copyright © 2025 Naif Al-Rasheed

All rights reserved. This book or any portion thereof may not be reproduced or used in any manner whatsoever without the express written permission of the publisher except for the use of brief quotations in a book review.

Cover and interior formatting designed by Sweet 'N Spicy Designs.

Print ISBN: 9798297039919

Contents

Introduction	v
IDENTIFYING AND SOURCING TURNAROUND OPPORTUNITIES	1
Strategic Partnerships and Networks	1
Market Analysis and Direct Outreach	2
Leveraging Professional Services and Government Initiatives	3
Additional Avenues	3
PHASE 1: ASSESSMENT	5
Detailed Diagnostic Analysis	9
Leveraging Formal Methodologies and Benchmarking	11
Financial Health Evaluation	13
Operational Performance Review	15
Sales and Marketing Assessment	16
PHASE 2: PLANNING	33
Developing Turnaround Strategies	34
Corporate Strategy and Business Model Realignment	37
Financial Restructuring and Capital Optimization	39
Operational Improvement Roadmaps	42
Sales and Marketing Turnaround Strategy	44
Organization and Workforce Plan (Human Capital)	50
Digital Transformation and IT Optimization	53
Stakeholder Communication and Change Management	57
Psychological Considerations in Phase 2 (Planning)	60
PHASE 3: IMPLEMENTATION	65
Executing Restructuring Plans	66
Monitoring and Performance Tracking	75
Leadership and Workforce Engagement	78
Risk Management and Contingency Planning	81
PHASE 4: SUSTAINABILITY AND GROWTH	88
Embedding Operational Excellence	92
Long-Term Financial Planning	97
Innovation and Market Expansion Strategies	102
Improvement and Agility Frameworks	109

AI INTEGRATION ACROSS TURNAROUND PHASES	116
Final Thoughts on the Complete Playbook	119
Case Studies	125
Appendix	142

Introduction

Overview

This playbook provides a structured, phased approach to transforming organizations (distressed or needs a corrective path) into sustainable, high-growth businesses. It is modeled on twenty-five years of experience investing in high-potential companies and executing turnarounds in high-stakes environments. It integrates top-tier strategy consulting frameworks with proven on-ground applications, ensuring each step is data-driven, actionable, and results-oriented.

Turnarounds require rebuilding a business under extreme uncertainty, operating under financial constraints, and executing with urgency to deliver results in compressed timelines. They demand resourceful, visionary leaders who are unafraid of making bold decisions.

Turnaround Priorities

1. **Crisis Management and Uncertainty as the Norm**
    - Turnarounds are often in uncharted waters, frequently lacking historical benchmarks or proven business models.

Turnarounds face financial distress, operational inefficiencies, and declining market share, where prior strategies have failed. They require rapid problem-solving and a willingness to pivot when conditions change.
2. **Speed of Execution and Adaptability**
   - Turnarounds must act fast to stabilize operations, regain profitability, and reestablish market confidence before cash runs out. Delayed action often leads to failure.
3. **Resource Constraints and Capital Efficiency**
   - Companies must maximize limited resources. Turnaround companies often operate with tight cash flows and lender scrutiny, requiring lean operations, creative financing strategies, and cost discipline to survive and scale.
4. **Building or Rebuilding Culture and Team Dynamics**
   - A turnaround must rebuild a broken or demoralized culture, instilling a sense of urgency, accountability, and shared purpose. The right team determines success.
5. **Winning Stakeholder Trust and Market Confidence**
   - In a turnaround, CEOs must rebuild trust with creditors, shareholders, suppliers, and employees, proving the company has a credible path forward. Storytelling, vision, and credibility are as crucial as operational execution.

Objectives and Scope

This playbook aims to equip leaders and change agents with a comprehensive roadmap for corporate turnarounds. It follows four key phases:

- **Assessment:** Diagnosing the root causes of distress and identifying opportunities
- **Planning:** Structuring a turnaround roadmap that aligns financial, operational, and cultural change
- **Implementation:** Driving execution, overcoming resistance, and ensuring immediate impact
- **Sustainability and Growth:** Embedding improvements, scaling transformation, and ensuring long-term success

Introduction

Each phase is grounded in theoretical underpinnings and practical execution strategies that worked in the past, making it applicable across manufacturing, services, technology, and industrial downstream sectors. Industry-specific insights and case studies illustrate how organizations can customize their approach to match market dynamics, leadership structure, and cultural context.

The content is designed to be highly structured and execution-focused, incorporating clear phases, checklists, deliverables, and KPIs to support executive decision-making. The playbook spans from immediate crisis stabilization to long-term strategic repositioning, ensuring that once a company is stabilized, the leader can begin building a long-lasting company that does not fall back into distress but pivots toward sustainable, competitive growth.

Approach: Each phase of the turnaround is broken down into key workstreams and deliverables, supported by both theoretical frameworks (e.g., Porter's Five Forces, Lean Six Sigma, Kotter's Change Management Principles) and actionable steps (e.g., 13-week cash flow modeling, AI-powered operational analytics, stakeholder communications plans).

Throughout the turnaround, the playbook emphasizes:

- Rigorous, data-driven analysis—diagnosing challenges with clear metrics and structured methodologies
- Execution discipline—ensuring leadership follows through on turnaround initiatives without getting stuck in over-analysis
- Empathetic leadership—recognizing that while financial restructuring is critical, transparent communication is essential to sustain morale, retain talent, and rebuild stakeholder trust

Many organizations mistakenly view turnarounds as purely financial or operational restructurings. This playbook challenges that notion. Turnaround success is not just about fixing broken balance sheets or cutting costs; it is about changing behaviors, rebuilding execution muscle, and embedding a culture of ownership and resilience.

Following this structured approach, leadership teams will be able to:

- Diagnose problems comprehensively.
- Design high-impact turnaround strategies.
- Implement change effectively and overcome resistance.
- Lock in gains through cultural and process reinforcements.

The end goal is not just to recover but to turn adversity into an opportunity. Many of the world's most successful companies, from Apple to AG&P, have gone through dramatic turnarounds before achieving market dominance. This playbook provides a structured approach to achieving that transformation.

Identifying and Sourcing Turnaround Opportunities

Identifying potential turnaround targets requires a proactive, *strategic search process*. This chapter outlines how organizations (or investors and change agents) can source distressed and/or turnaround required but promising companies using a multi-channel approach:

Strategic Partnerships and Networks

Collaborate with banks, financial institutions, and advisory firms to tap into early leads on troubled companies. Many turnaround opportunities surface via financial stakeholders, such as banks' special assets units or private equity firms specializing in distress. Building relationships with such entities provides a pipeline of candidates. Additionally, engage industry associations and chambers of commerce to stay informed on member companies facing difficulties; these organizations often quietly seek help for struggling constituents. Networking within private equity associations is another avenue—it connects you with professionals who may refer you to opportunities.

The underlying strategy is to create an ecosystem where referrals and early warnings about underperforming businesses become readily available. A classic case is how investors partnered with governments during the 2008 financial crisis to identify banks or industrial firms in need. Those partnerships provided vetted targets for turnaround with stakeholder support from day one. An actual example from KSA is their economic slowdown in 2017. The private sector stimulus office, where I established a small bailout fund for companies struggling, reached out to the banks. We worked closely with them to identify and approach companies that could help them with distressing situations. We asked them for turnaround plans, KPIs, and specific measures, which are outlined in some phases in this book. That helped my team identify and back only strong companies with solid management and sound planning.

Market Analysis and Direct Outreach

Conduct *proactive market scanning* to pinpoint sectors under duress (e.g., an industry facing technological disruption or commodity price downturn). By analyzing industry reports and financial filings, a turnaround team can identify companies with distress signals, such as consecutive losses, shrinking margins, high industrial leverage, or debt covenant breaches. For instance, in the oil and gas downstream sector, a drop in oil prices in 2014 flagged several refinery and petrochemical firms at risk of bankruptcy. The proactive analysis identified those with strong core assets but temporary financial strain. After analysis, execute a *direct outreach strategy*: discreetly approach target companies' owners or executives with a value proposition for partnership.

Position the turnaround team as problem solvers who bring fresh capital, management expertise, or restructuring plans. Direct outreach must be sensitive. Often, confidentiality and timing are critical. Right after a weak earnings report or leadership change, a well-timed approach can open doors to negotiation before competitors swoop in. In summary, combining data-driven market analysis with a tactful direct approach helps secure *exclusive turnaround opportunities* before they officially seek help, thereby avoiding having to enter into an auction-style competition.

Leveraging Professional Services and Government Initiatives

Utilize insights from legal, accounting, executive search firms, and consulting firms that specialize in restructuring. Advisory firms often become aware of companies on the brink through engagements that didn't proceed or companies shopping for help. Establishing connections here can lead to an *early-mover advantage* on deals. Likewise, stay attuned to government programs or investment initiatives targeting struggling industries, such as government privatization lists or public-private partnership programs where underperforming state enterprises are being opened to turnaround investors.

We had a similar experience with the government in the Philippines, and it was one of the most successful turnaround situations I have been involved in. In Saudi Arabia, leveraging bodies such as the Ministry of Investment (MISA) or the Public Investment Fund (PIF) can reveal targets aligned with national transformation priorities (e.g., a state-owned manufacturing firm that needs restructuring to meet Vision 2030 goals). Government tenders or bailout programs might become available for distressed firms in strategic sectors, such as airlines or utilities, providing a channel to step in as a turnaround sponsor with public backing. In essence, *aligning with government initiatives* can uncover opportunities and can also offer political and financial support mechanisms to increase the chances of turnaround success.

Additional Avenues

Public Signals and Events

Beyond networks and analysis, monitor *public records and market signals* for distress. CMA-required regulatory filings and other sources, like the bankruptcy committee at the Ministry of Commerce, are rich sources of warning signs. Similarly, negative press or *corporate governance issues* (auditor resignations, sudden CEO departures, or a new CEO search) often precede a company's decline and present an opening for turnaround proposals. Concurrently, attend industry conferences, trade shows, and investment summits, like the Future Investment Initiative in Riyadh, where you can network with executives and investors. Informal conversations at these events often reveal companies quietly seeking help or willing to divest troubled divisions. Maintaining high visibility in such forums makes turnaround investors become "go-to" contacts when crises emerge. In summary, casting a wide net—from media monitoring to conference networking—ensures you won't miss the subtle early signs that a company could be your next successful turnaround project.

Phase 1: Assessment

Phase 1 Overview: Phase 1 is an in-depth assessment of the company's current state. It begins with immediate stabilization of the business (particularly cash) and then a comprehensive diagnostic across all facets of the organization. This phase is critical for identifying *the root causes of underperformance*: distinguishing between symptoms (e.g., cash crunch) and fundamental problems (e.g., loss-making product lines or dysfunctional culture). The assessment covers strategy, financials, operations, market position, organizational health, and external factors. By the end of Phase 1, the turnaround team should have a clear fact base: *what went wrong, where, and why?*

Equally important, Phase 1 sets the tone for the turnaround. Early wins in stabilizing the company build credibility, and thorough analysis builds a case for change. This is also where leadership must confront brutal facts while maintaining morale. Often, troubled companies suffer from a culture of denial or finger-pointing. An effective assessment phase counteracts this by promoting open dialogue around issues. For example, Rosabeth Moss Kanter describes how distressed companies fall into a "death spiral" of blame, silos, helplessness, and ultimately denial.

In Phase 1, the new leadership should break that cycle by fostering transparency and collaboration from the start. Simply put, *acknowledging problems is the first step to solving them*. A famous historical parallel is Lou Gerstner's turnaround of IBM. Upon joining in 1993, he spent months conducting intensive assessments, openly listening to employees and customers about IBM's problems before formulating a plan. Startup founders face similar challenges in that they need to foster values like transparency and regular communication to gain support, encourage creativity, and allow buy-ins from those who quit their jobs to join a new company, taking a considerable risk. By doing so, they built trust and ensured the plan addressed real issues. At the end of Phase 1, you will have a diagnostic report and a galvanized team ready for action in Phase 2.

Immediate Cash Flow Stabilization and Triage (first two to four weeks)

Before diving into complete diagnostics, *securing short-term liquidity* and stopping any bleeding is imperative. In a turnaround, *cash is oxygen*. Without stabilizing cash flow, deeper analysis or restructuring can't proceed. This subphase often runs in parallel with data gathering for the assessment. Key actions include:

- **Set Up a Cash War Room**

  Immediately establish a dedicated team (often led by a Chief Restructuring Officer or CFO) responsible for daily cash management. The "war room" operates with top management's oversight and meets *daily* to review cash inflows, outflows, and balances. All discretionary spending authority is centralized here, effectively *holding the checkbook* to control every dollar. By implementing a thirteen-week rolling cash flow forecast (a best practice tool in turnarounds), the team maps out the company's cash trajectory under the best, base, and worst-case scenarios. This proactive monitoring enables quick decisions (like delaying payables or accelerating collections) to avert a crisis. The war room also communicates cash status to stakeholders (e.g., lenders) to build confidence that the situation is under control.

- **Expense Freeze and Quick Cost Cuts**

As an immediate measure, *freeze all non-essential operating expenses* for a brief period (often thirty days). This includes halting travel, pausing uncommitted marketing spending, and deferring optional maintenance, among other measures. The rationale is to conserve cash until a plan is in place. Simultaneously, identify "low-hanging fruit" cost cuts, such as ending contractors/consultants, cutting executive perks, or renegotiating a major vendor contract for a short-term discount. These quick cuts send a signal to the organization that *cost discipline is the new norm* and can free up cash within weeks.

We encountered a similar situation when we took over Duet management in India, essentially holding all spending and centralizing the checkbook to one person. We leveraged another portfolio company's supplier chain in China to ensure operational continuity. We halted the contract with the OEM while we developed a comprehensive plan for the future to turn the company around. Such swift actions generated liquidity and funded the critical early stages of the turnaround.

• **Accelerate Receivables and Release Working Capital**

Improving cash isn't just about cutting costs—it's also about bringing cash in faster. Launch a focused effort to *collect outstanding receivables* (e.g., offer early payment discounts or intensify collection calls on overdue accounts). For urgent cases, consider factoring receivables (selling invoices for immediate cash) as a temporary solution, albeit at a financing cost. Simultaneously, *liquidate idle working capital*: if high inventory is tying up cash, initiate clearance sales or negotiate returns to suppliers. In a manufacturing firm, for instance, selling off slow-moving or excess stock can yield a quick cash injection. Even at a discount, cash now may be worth more than inventory on hand. Additionally, work with procurement to delay noncritical purchases and use existing inventory. These steps can shorten the cash conversion cycle and add precious liquidity.

• **Secure Short-Term Financing (if needed):**

If internal measures are insufficient to stabilize cash, prepare for *temporary financing solutions*. This could include drawing down existing credit lines, approaching banks or asset-based lenders for bridge loans, or negotiating customer prepayments. In some cases, emergency equity injections from owners might be necessary to prevent insolvency. (This applies to companies owned by the government or with large outstanding debts to the government.) Transparency with current lenders is crucial: proactively inform them of the situation and the turnaround plan underway. The goal is to *buy time* and ensure the company can fund payroll and critical expenses during the turnaround. Any new funding obtained should be used judiciously under the war room's oversight, with final checkbook signatory rules established, typically with a single person (the CEO) in charge, and with a clear payback or exit strategy defined once the turnaround yields results.

Key Actions:

- Set Up a Cash "War Room"
    - Hold the checkbook final signatory.
    - Establish a War Room Committee comprising key personnel from the company, including the CRO, CFO, and treasurer, if applicable.
    - Empower the team's CRO, CFO, and treasurer to track daily cash inflows/ outflows.
    - Use a thirteen-week rolling cash flow model with best, base, and worst-case scenarios (McKinsey, 2019).
- Expense Freeze and Quick Cost Cuts
    - Freeze nonessential OpEx (travel, marketing, discretionary R&D) for an initial fifteen-to-thirty-day review.
    - Identify quick, high-cost items and immediate vendor renegotiations, focusing on high-cost contracts with flexible terms.
- AR Acceleration and Working Capital Release
    - Expedite receivables through early payment discounts or factoring only if there is an immediate cash need situation.
    - If feasible, reduce raw material or finished goods inventory (e.g., reorder quantity rationalization).
- Short-Term Financing Options
    - If needed, secure temporary bridge financing (private lenders, asset-based loans, or, if the mandate is approved, one

Phase 1: Assessment

of the credit financial institutions) to avert insolvency triggers.
- Communicate with existing lenders about potential near-term covenant breaches to prevent default and enable you to provide a plan to turn around the company.
- These emergency measures stabilize the company's liquidity, allowing the subsequent Phase 1: Detailed Diagnostic Analysis to proceed without risking an immediate cash crisis.

Detailed Diagnostic Analysis

Once immediate stability is addressed, the team conducts a thorough diagnostic analysis across all business dimensions. This diagnostic is akin to a comprehensive health check-up of the company, identifying problems and opportunities in detail:

- **Corporate Strategy Assessment:** Evaluate the company's strategic direction in relation to market reality. Are the current *mission* and *vision* aligned with the market needs and the company's core strengths? Often in times of distress, strategy has drifted or become incoherent. Perform a *market position analysis*, e.g., use *Porter's Five Forces* to understand competitive pressures and analyze where the company stands relative to rivals (market share trends, customer perceptions). Identify if there's a clear *value proposition* or if the company is stuck in the middle (neither low-cost nor differentiated). Check for adjacency or diversification moves that failed: are there non-core businesses draining resources? The output is a concise appraisal of whether the company's strategy contributed to its distress (for instance, over-expansion, incorrect market focus) and what strategic options exist moving forward (e.g., refocusing on core, pursuing a niche, etc.). *Benchmarking* is useful here: compare the company's strategic metrics (growth, R&D spending, product mix) to those of healthier competitors to identify gaps. This strategic diagnostic guides the big choices in Phase 2 planning.

- **Financial Health Evaluation:** Perform a deep dive into financial statements to assess viability. Analyze liquidity (cash levels, current ratio) to understand short-term survival prospects. Examine leverage and debt covenants: are any breaches imminent, and what is the debt maturity profile? A distressed firm often has an overleveraged balance sheet, so quantifying the *debt reduction needed* (via restructuring or asset sales) is key. Evaluate profitability by segment to see which products or units are loss-making. Conduct a cost structure analysis: fixed versus variable costs, overhead as a percentage of sales versus industry benchmarks, and, my favorite, the industrial leverage ratio. This indicates whether the company is bloated in SG&A or suffering poor gross margins. Also, review cash flow from operations: is working capital management efficient, or are inventory and accounts receivable consuming cash? The financial diagnostic should produce a clear picture of the *baseline financial health* and help set targets (e.g., "We need to cut costs by 20 percent" or "We need to renegotiate debt covenants to avoid default"). It also feeds into immediate actions. For example, if specific contracts, business lines, and/or assets are unprofitable, those become candidates for cut or closure in Phase 2.

• **Operational Performance Review:** Analyze core operations to identify inefficiencies in production or service delivery. In manufacturing companies, this involves examining key metrics such as capacity utilization, yield, scrap rates, cycle times, and OEE (Overall Equipment Effectiveness). Are plants underutilized or plagued by downtime, or are bottlenecks present? Is quality control causing high rework or returns? Do we need to reestablish specific actions, such as quality checks before bottling a medicine, for example? Map the value stream to pinpoint bottlenecks: perhaps one stage of production is throttling the entire output. In service businesses, assess process flow (e.g., hospital patient wait times or a software firm's customer onboarding time).

Identify any service-level lapses (like high customer churn or complaints) indicating broken processes. Scrutinize the supply chain: are there unreliable suppliers or excess inventory due to poor demand forecasting? This operational audit often reveals both quick fixes (process tweaks) and larger needs, such as capital investment or system upgrades. For example, if a plant is only at 50 percent capacity due to outdated equipment, a turnaround might involve consolidating facilities or investing in maintenance. The operational review yields a list of efficiency improvement opportunities and helps explain how operational issues contributed to financial distress (e.g., high costs, late deliveries, losing customers, etc.).

- **Market Position and Competitor Analysis:** Examine the company's external environment. How is the company performing in its market relative to competitors? This involves examining *market share trends, customer segments, pricing strategy,* and *marketing effectiveness.* Perhaps the company lost market share because a competitor introduced a superior product or a disruptive technology changed the industry. Conduct a competitor benchmarking compare product offerings, pricing, customer service, and innovation pace. Analyze customer feedback and brand perception: Is the company seen as a laggard? Interview key customers or sales team members to examine why deals are won or lost.

Additionally, consider broader industry trends, such as a shift to digital channels or regulatory changes that might erode the company's advantage. Identify any "quick win" opportunities like underserved niches or customer pain points that competitors aren't addressing, which the company could exploit post-turnaround. Understanding the market position grounds the turnaround in reality: it ensures the plan (Phase 2) addresses internal issues and how the company will regain a competitive edge externally. For example, Starbucks' assessment in 2008 recognized that overexpansion had diluted the customer experience, and competitors and the financial crisis were changing consumer habits (brownandjoseph.com). This insight led them to refocus on core customers and experience in the turnaround plan.

Leveraging Formal Methodologies and Benchmarking

- **Benchmarking**: Compare the company's financial and operational KPIs with industry-wide data to quantify performance gaps (BCG, *Benchmarks for Distressed Companies,* 2020). For example, if industry overhead averages 18 percent of revenue and the company's overhead is at 26 percent, this signals an 8 percent overhead reduction target.

- **Root-Cause Analysis Tools**: Employ the "Five Whys" or a "Fishbone

(Ishikawa) Diagram" to drill down on major cost or revenue shortfalls (KPMG, *Root Cause Analysis in Restructuring*, 2022).

During the assessment phase, organizational psychology is pivotal in enabling or hindering honest diagnosis. When a new turnaround team arrives, employees are typically anxious and defensive: fear of layoffs or blame can cause information hoarding or an optimistic glossing over of problems. Leaders must create an atmosphere of trust and candor from the outset. This can be achieved by clearly communicating that the purpose of the assessment is to identify issues collectively and save the company, rather than assigning individual blame. Quick, visible actions, such as the cash war room, can paradoxically boost morale and raise engagement: employees see that a plan is in motion to address the crisis, reducing uncertainty. It's important to engage key managers in the diagnostic process (e.g., involve department heads in analyzing their areas) so they feel part of the solution and not simply judged. However, developing a war room is also tricky. It requires a highly experienced project manager to understand from the CEO where to build momentum and how to break down tasks and milestones.

Deliverables:

- **SWOT Analysis Document**: This document provides a clear breakdown of internal strengths and weaknesses, as well as external opportunities and threats. It will serve as a strategic checkpoint, ensuring that turnaround initiatives align with existing competitive advantages while addressing fundamental weaknesses. The SWOT is especially critical for assessing whether the business model remains viable in its current market.
- **Strategic Alignment Scorecard**: This scorecard evaluates whether the company's initiatives align with its long-term strategic objectives. It highlights gaps where resources are misallocated and provides a quantitative assessment of misalignment. This tool will be key in Phase 2 when prioritizing which projects or business units to focus on or divest from.
- **Benchmarking and Comparable Report**: This report compares the company's financial and operational performance with that of

Phase 1: Assessment

its industry peers. It includes profitability metrics, efficiency benchmarks, and comparative analyses of competitors. The purpose is to provide an objective baseline, ensuring that performance targets set in the turnaround plan are grounded in industry best practices.

Financial Health Evaluation

- **Financial Analysis**
    - Purpose: Identify financial health, liquidity, and structural risks.
    - Liquidity review: Assessing liquidity involves analyzing cash flow statements to identify pressures and forecast potential shortfalls. A thirteen-week rolling cash flow model should be used to evaluate short-term solvency.
    - Stress-test cash reserves under various scenarios: The company must stress-test different scenarios, such as delayed receivables, supplier payment demands, and unexpected costs. If liquidity risk is high, leadership may need to initiate emergency cost-cutting or secure bridge financing.

- **Debt and Covenant Analysis:**
    - Review loan agreements, covenant breaches, and upcoming maturities: Reviewing loan agreements, interest obligations, and covenant restrictions is critical in determining restructuring needs. Debt covenants that restrict operational flexibility should be flagged for renegotiation.
    - Assess interest coverage and leverage ratios against industry benchmarks to ensure alignment. If leverage levels exceed industry norms, options such as refinancing, debt-for-equity swaps, or structured payment extensions should be explored.

- **Profitability Analysis:**
    - Segment profitability by product, region, or service to identify high- and low-margin areas: Understanding which business segments drive profitability helps prioritize restructuring

efforts. The company should segment financial performance by product, geography, or customer type, identifying areas with negative margins.
- **Cost Structure Evaluation:**
  - Identify fixed versus variable costs.
  - Evaluate overhead efficiency, particularly in manufacturing (e.g., plant utilization). Overhead costs must also be reviewed to determine inefficiencies, such as excess labor or redundant facilities.

Deliverables:

- **Comprehensive Financial Dashboard**: This real-time dashboard consolidates key financial metrics (revenue, profitability, working capital, and debt ratios) in one place. It is a monitoring tool that enables leadership to track financial recovery as the turnaround progresses.

Twelve-Month Liquidity Projection: A rolling cash flow model maps out expected inflows and outflows under different scenarios to support financial planning. This is crucial in determining whether short-term financing, restructuring, or asset sales are required.

- **Debt Restructuring Risk Matrix**: This risk assessment categorizes outstanding debts based on urgency, default risk, and potential renegotiation strategies. It provides a roadmap for debt restructuring negotiations.
- **Industrial Leverage Report**: This analysis compares the company's leverage ratios with industry norms. It highlights where debt levels are unsustainable and suggests strategies for reducing financial risk.

Operational Performance Review

Operational Assessment

Purpose: Identify inefficiencies in production, service delivery, and supply chains.

- Manufacturing industry-Specific Assessment:
    - Production Data Analysis: Analyze WIP levels between stations to identify accumulation points.
    - Value Stream Mapping: Map detailed process flows with timing to identify bottlenecks and optimize workflow.
    - Capacity Utilization: Compare heoreticcal versus actual throughput at each station.
    - Equipment Effectiveness: Track performance by measuring overall equipment effectiveness across all machinery.
    - Quality Control: Review defect rates and warranty claims to identify and address quality issues.
    - Lean Manufacturing: Evaluate waste reduction opportunities and perform constraint analysis to streamline production, reduce waste, and increase efficiency. For example, the pharmaceutical industry production implements quality checks before the bottling line to prevent processing batches that will be rejected later.
- Service Industry-Specific Assessment (Healthcare Sector example):
- Patient Flow Analysis: Track wait times between stages of care delivery.
- Customer Retention: Analyze churn rates and service feedback to identify areas for improvement. Ensure this is done unbiasedly and select the correct representation of the population, with critical involvement by the lead turnaround manager.
- Resources Utilization: Measure equipment and specialist availability versus demand.
- Capacity Versus Demand Modeling: Develop theoretical models based on actual patient volumes.

- Scalability: Identify bottlenecks in resource allocation or customer onboarding.
- Supply Chain Review:
    - Identify supplier dependencies and vulnerabilities.
    - Evaluate inventory management practices (e.g., JIT, buffer stock).
    - Perform an operational flow and bottlenecks analysis.
    - Track a cost-per-unit or service delivery efficiency scorecard.
    - Analyze risk assessment for supplier reliability.

Sales and Marketing Assessment

Purpose: Assess the effectiveness of customer acquisition, retention, and brand positioning.

- Customer Analysis:
    - Customers should be segmented based on their lifetime value, churn risk, and acquisition cost. Special attention must be paid to contractual renewal rates and the effectiveness of loyalty programs. Customer confidence issues must be addressed if distress negatively impacts brand perception. (This also depends on the industry.) Market segmentation can also be conducted by gender, age, life expectancy, socioeconomic status (rich/poor), benefit sought segmentation, systematic and/or product-related behavior, and whether the purchase is made online or in-store.
    - Review existing loyalty programs, customer service responsiveness, and contract renewal rates to pinpoint weaknesses in retaining customers during periods of turmoil.
    - Identify unprofitable customer relationships and analyze the reasons.
    - Recognize opportunities for bundling, cross-selling, or dropping high-maintenance customers.
- Sales Performance:
    - Evaluate the pipeline conversion rates and salesforce productivity.

Phase 1: Assessment

- Assess pricing flexibility and discounting practices.
- Benchmark against competitors.
- Marketing Efficiency
    - Analyze the return on investment (ROI) of marketing campaigns.
    - Customer Confidence Check: Analyze customer feedback and churn indicators to identify if news of the company's distress is affecting customer behavior. Include a brand sentiment review (monitoring press, social media, and client inquiries) to identify any erosion of trust or reputation issues that require immediate attention.
    - Evaluate the effectiveness of digital versus traditional marketing.

Deliverables:

- **Customer Profitability Analysis**: Identifies which customer segments generate the most profit. This analysis enables strategic focus on high-value clients while eliminating unprofitable accounts.
- **Brand Positioning Report**: Analyzes the brand's perception in the market compared to competitors. This includes brand sentiment tracking and potential repositioning strategies.
- **Sales Pipeline and Lead Conversion Report:** Evaluates the effectiveness of the sales funnel, from lead generation to closed deals. It highlights inefficiencies and opportunities for optimization.
- **Marketing ROI Dashboard:** Measures the performance of different marketing channels. This dashboard ensures budget allocation is optimized for maximum return.

Human Resources and Organizational Culture Assessment

Purpose: Understand talent gaps, organizational culture, and leadership alignment.

- Leadership Evaluation:

- Assess leadership effectiveness, accountability, and vision alignment.
- Review succession planning.
- Leadership Bench Strength:
  - Decision-Making Audit: Evaluate the leadership team's decision-making speed and effectiveness under pressure. Identify whether critical decisions have been delayed or avoided and gauge the leadership's openness to change. Determine whether the management culture is too centralized (causing bottlenecks) or chaotic (lack of apparent authority), as this will inform the turnaround plan.
  - Mindset and Morale: Interview key executives to understand their level of buy-in or denial regarding the company's issues. This "soft audit" of leadership psychology can reveal if leaders are resistant to external advice, which could impede turnaround efforts.
- Talent Audit:
  - Identify skill gaps, overstaffing, or understaffing in critical departments.
  - Assess employee turnover and engagement metrics.
  - Culture Assessment:
  - Conduct employee surveys to gauge morale and resistance to change.
  - Identify cultural misalignments that hinder innovation or execution.

Deliverables:

- **Leadership Competency Matrix:** assesses leadership strengths and gaps, ensuring the turnaround plan is backed by the right talent.
- **Workforce Optimization Report:** analyzes whether the organization is overstaffed or understaffed in key areas, guiding restructuring efforts.
- **Cultural Alignment Heatmap:** identifies cultural strengths and resistance points, helping to tailor change management strategies.

Phase 1: Assessment

IT and Digital Infrastructure Assessment

Purpose: Identify *technology inefficiencies* and assess opportunities for *digital transformation*, improving system reliability, security, and automation.

- System Efficiency:
    - An organization's enterprise systems (ERP, CRM, HRM) *must be assessed for usability, integration gaps, and scalability.* Many legacy systems operate in silos, leading to data inconsistencies and inefficiencies. Evaluating interoperability between business functions (finance, supply chain, customer service) is critical. Bottlenecks in manual processes should be identified to explore opportunities for automation, thereby reducing workload redundancy and improving efficiency.
    - Using AI: Companies that leverage machine learning-powered ERP systems improve operational efficiency by up to 40 percent (HBR AI Reports). AI enhances real-time decision-making by reducing forecasting errors and supply chain mismanagement. AI-powered predictive maintenance also prevents downtime, increasing system uptime and reliability. Using RPA (Robotic Process Automation) to automate repetitive tasks such as invoicing and data reconciliation can reduce overhead by 30 percent to 50 percent.
- Cybersecurity and Data Management:
    - Cybersecurity is a significant concern, particularly for organizations undergoing a turnaround where financial vulnerabilities make them a target for cyber threats. A cybersecurity audit should assess the company's ability to withstand phishing attacks, ransomware, and internal breaches.
    - Using AI: AI-based threat detection systems can predict and prevent cyberattacks in real-time, reducing breaches by 60 percent, according to a recent Palantir study. AI-driven *zero-trust security models* enhance access control, reducing

unauthorized data exposure. Data accuracy issues must also be addressed, particularly in financial reporting and customer databases, where inaccuracies can disrupt turnaround efforts.
- Digital Transformation Readiness:
  - Organizations must assess their readiness to integrate AI, analytics, and IoT to improve decision-making and operational efficiency. Key questions include:
    1. Does the company have real-time data collection for decision-making?
    2. Are employees digitally skilled to work alongside AI-powered tools?
    3. Can automation reduce operational costs and human dependency?
    4. AI-powered predictive analytics can optimize supply chains, reducing waste and inefficiencies. IoT-enabled smart factories cut downtime by 30 percent and increase productivity. AI-driven customer experience tools improve retention by 20 percent through personalized insights.

Deliverables:

- **IT Efficiency Scorecard:** measures system reliability, downtime, and integration issues
- **Cybersecurity Vulnerability Report:** identifies risks in the company's IT infrastructure and suggests mitigation strategies
- **AI-based Threat Monitoring and Data Verification Systems:** safeguard sensitive business information
- **Digital Transformation Roadmap:** outlines steps for modernizing IT systems, automating processes, and leveraging analytics for business intelligence
- **AI-Based IT System Audit Report:** maps inefficiencies and prioritizes automation
- **Digital Transformation Roadmap:** provides a twelve-month structured AI-integration plan

Phase 1: Assessment

External Market Environment Assessment

Purpose: A company does not operate in isolation. External market conditions, including industry trends, economic shifts, geopolitical risks, and competitive pressures, influence its success or failure. Understanding these external forces allows leadership to proactively identify opportunities and mitigate threats during a turnaround. This assessment is crucial for shaping adaptive strategies that ensure long-term viability.

- Industry Trends:
    - Identifying Disruptive Trends
        - Industries are constantly evolving due to technological advancements, regulatory changes, and shifts in consumer behavior. Companies undergoing turnaround must analyze whether they are lagging behind in adopting critical industry innovations or if new entrants are disrupting their market share.
        - For example, in manufacturing, the rise of Industry 4.0 (AI-driven automation, IoT-enabled factories, and predictive maintenance) has reshaped operational efficiency. A company relying on legacy production methods will struggle to compete with AI-powered competitors that dynamically optimize production costs and efficiencies. Similarly, e-commerce and AI-powered recommendation engines have altered the traditional dynamics of brick-and-mortar retail.
        - Additionally, government regulations or industry-wide compliance requirements, such as carbon neutrality targets in industrial sectors, can force companies to pivot their strategies. A failure to adapt to sustainability regulations could result in supply chain disruptions, legal liabilities, or investor pressure.
        - A thorough analysis of these macro trends ensures that turnaround strategies align with future market realities rather than relying solely on short-term survival tactics.

- Market Growth or Contraction Forecasts
  - Market expansion or contraction influences investment decisions, product strategies, and operational priorities. A company should assess:
    - Projected demand trends in its sector. For instance, cost-cutting and niche specialization might be the best approach if the industry is expected to shrink by 5 percent annually. Conversely, if the sector is growing, strategic repositioning and investment in innovation could yield high returns.
    - Consumer behavior shifts: Do changing demographics or digital transformation trends threaten traditional revenue streams?
    - Supply and demand fluctuations: For industrial companies, commodity price volatility erodes margins or creates sourcing issues.
    - Investment activity in the sector: Are private equity firms investing in similar turnarounds? If so, securing funding might be more feasible.
    - By analyzing these growth indicators, companies can align restructuring efforts with long-term industry prospects, ensuring they don't invest in declining markets or miss expansion opportunities.

Geopolitical and Economic Risks:

Currency Risks, Trade Barriers, and Inflationary Pressures

Global economic conditions directly impact a company's cost structure, supply chain, and pricing power. Key risk areas include:

1. Currency Volatility: Exchange rate fluctuations can affect import/export costs, making operations unpredictable. Companies should employ hedging strategies to protect against major swings.
2. Trade Barriers and Tariffs: Protectionist policies, trade disputes, and supply chain disruptions (e.g., post-COVID logistics crises) impact sourcing strategies and profitability. Companies relying on

Phase I: Assessment

global suppliers must evaluate regional alternatives to avoid cost spikes.
3. Inflation and Interest Rates: Rising costs of raw materials, logistics, and financing can erode margins. Companies should lock in supplier contracts, negotiate favorable payment terms, and explore cost pass-through mechanisms to protect profitability.
4. A turnaround strategy must account for these macroeconomic risks, ensuring financial planning incorporates scenario modeling for worst-case inflationary shocks, currency devaluation risks, and potential tariff hikes.

Dependencies on High-Risk Suppliers and Regions

A single high-risk supplier or overreliance on a specific region can threaten business continuity. Examples include:

- Tech companies rely on semiconductor suppliers in Taiwan or China, where geopolitical tensions could disrupt chip supply chains.
- Retail brands source from a single country prone to labor strikes, which causes a lack of diversification and inventory shortages.
- Industrial firms depend on fluctuating oil prices without proper hedging tools. Profit margins may be unstable if a company's raw materials are linked to energy price volatility.

To mitigate risks, businesses should conduct a supplier diversification analysis, exploring options such as onshoring, nearshoring, or multi-vendor partnerships to spread geopolitical exposure. This assessment ensures the turnaround strategy fortifies supply chain resilience rather than just cutting costs.

Competitor Benchmarks:

Comparing Performance Metrics, Cost Structures, and Strategic Initiatives

Competitive benchmarking provides a realistic performance gauge by comparing the following

- Profit margins and cost structures: Is the company spending more on operations or supply chain than industry benchmarks?
  - Market share erosion: Have competitors launched AI-powered products, aggressive pricing models, or partnerships that weakened the company's position?
  - Investment and R&D focus: Are rivals allocating resources to automation, digital transformation, or emerging markets?

For example, it is likely underperforming if competitors have adopted predictive AI-driven customer analytics, but the company continues to use outdated manual forecasting. Similarly, if competitors optimize supply chains with AI-driven logistics, but the company faces high inventory costs and inefficiencies, the turnaround strategy should prioritize digital adoption.

Benchmarking allows the turnaround CEO to prioritize corrective actions in underperforming areas while identifying potential competitive advantages to leverage.

Deliverables:

i. **Industry Disruption Matrix:** a visual representation of technological, regulatory, and economic disruptions affecting the company's market position
ii. **Competitor Benchmarking Report:** a side-by-side analysis comparing financial performance, innovation strategies, and cost structures with industry leaders
iii. **Economic Risk Scenario Analysis:** forecasting potential impacts of currency risks, inflation, and geopolitical instability on financial performance.

Governance and Compliance Assessment

Purpose: Governance failures often lead to mismanagement, regulatory violations, and investor distrust—all amplifying business distress. A turnaround must strengthen corporate governance, ensure compliance, and rebuild stakeholder confidence.

a. Regulatory Compliance:
   i. Ensuring Legal and Industry-Specific Compliance

A company under financial distress often overlooks regulatory requirements, leading to legal liabilities, operational shutdowns, or public PR crises. The assessment should review the following:

- Licensing and Certifications: Are industry certifications (ISO, CMA licenses, or environmental permits) up to date? Noncompliance can block market access or result in substantial fines.
- Labor and Safety Laws: Are workforce regulations (working hours, health and safety, wage laws) adhered to? Noncompliance can result in shutdowns or lawsuits in sectors such as manufacturing or oil and gas.
- Tax and Financial Reporting: Are financial records transparent and accurate? Turnarounds often reveal accounting irregularities (overstated revenues, tax liabilities) that require immediate rectification.

b. Corporate Governance:
   i. Board Effectiveness and Strategic Oversight

Weak governance structures allow poor leadership decisions, strategic misalignment, and a lack of accountability to persist. Assessing governance involves:

- Board Composition and Expertise: Does the board have members with turnaround experience or expertise in critical areas (finance, operations, technology)? Companies in crisis often lack external advisors, leading to strategic blind spots.
- Decision-Making and Oversight: Are major investments, cost-cutting decisions, and restructuring plans reviewed transparently? If executives control decision-making without proper board scrutiny, risks increase.

- Investor and Shareholder Confidence: Are governance structures transparent? Poor governance can deter investors from supporting recapitalization efforts.

Turnaround success relies on robust corporate oversight, ensuring financial and strategic decisions align with stakeholder interests. Ideal and best practices recommend that specific committees be in place at this stage. There should be at least eight committees with various stakeholders overseeing critical issues, such as the Operational Risk and Procurement Committee and the HR and Culture Committee.

Deliverables:

i. **Compliance Audit Checklist:** documents regulatory compliance status and identifies any risks
ii. **Corporate Governance Maturity Assessment:** evaluates governance structures, transparency, and accountability levels

Stakeholder Engagement Analysis

Purpose: A successful turnaround is not just about financial and operational restructuring—it also requires effective stakeholder engagement. Internal and external stakeholders have vested interests in the company's recovery, and their alignment (or resistance) can either accelerate or derail the process. By understanding the priorities, concerns, and influence of different stakeholders, leadership can create a strategic engagement plan to gain trust, manage expectations, and drive collaboration.

Internal Stakeholders:

1. Gauging Executive and Employee Readiness for Change
    i. Executives and employees play a crucial role in executing a turnaround strategy, but their readiness to adapt varies widely. Assessing leadership and workforce sentiment is critical because:
        - Executives may resist restructuring if it threatens existing power dynamics. Some may fear job losses, reputational risks, or loss of control. Others may be in denial about the company's distress, which can slow down decision-making.

- Employees face uncertainty and morale challenges, especially if layoffs, cultural shifts, or new operational processes are introduced. Without clarity, productivity can decline, and attrition may increase.

To address these risks, leadership should conduct confidential surveys, town halls, and one-on-one interviews to gauge concerns and prepare an internal communication strategy that fosters transparency, trust, and buy-in. Employees and executives must understand the rationale behind the turnaround and their role in the company's future vision.

2. Identifying Potential Internal Resistance Points
    - Turnaround efforts often encounter active and passive resistance from internal stakeholders. Resistance typically manifests in three ways:
        - Operational Resistance: Mid-level managers and frontline employees may hesitate to adopt new business processes, cost-cutting measures, or performance targets. This is common when workforce reductions increase workloads or existing processes are deeply ingrained in the organization.
        - Cultural Resistance: If the company shifts its strategic focus (e.g., moving from traditional retail to digital channels), employees may feel ill-equipped to adapt to new expectations. A cultural misalignment between leadership and teams can cause friction.
        - Leadership Silos and Misalignment: Executives who benefited from old business models may resist radical change. Conflicts among leadership teams can create decision paralysis, slowing down the implementation process.

Mitigation strategies include change management programs, executive coaching, and incentive realignment to ensure leaders and employees embrace the transformation rather than undermine it.

3. External Stakeholders

- Engaging Lenders, Investors, and Suppliers to Assess Flexibility and Concerns

External stakeholders—especially creditors, investors, and suppliers—are critical to ensuring financial stability during a turnaround. Misalignment with these stakeholders can create liquidity crises, supplier disruptions, or investor distrust. The company must assess:

- Lender and Creditor Flexibility: If the company is in financial distress, lenders must be engaged early to renegotiate terms, extend repayment periods, or provide bridge financing. Turnaround CEOs should prepare a debt restructuring roadmap to show how the company will regain solvency.
- Investor Sentiment and Capital Access: Institutional and private investors need confidence in the new leadership's strategy. The turnaround plan must outline clear revenue paths, cost optimizations, and competitive repositioning to attract continued or new investment and engage those stakeholders as part of a wider communication strategy for the company.
- Supplier Commitments and Contract Adjustments: When suppliers fear payment delays, operational risks, or potential customer loss, they may react by reducing credit terms, severing contracts, or diverting resources to other competitors, particularly in cases when there is a historical strategic relationship. Proactively renegotiating supplier agreements can ensure the continuity of materials, services, or distribution channels. Companies can stabilize critical relationships and build trust in the turnaround process by conducting structured stakeholder negotiations.

Understanding Customer Expectations During the Transition

A failing company often loses customer confidence, and if this isn't addressed in the communication strategy, revenue recovery will be delayed. Customers may be concerned about service quality, product availability, or the long-term viability of the company. The assessment should identify:

- Customer Retention Risks: Are major customers considering switching to competitors due to instability? What measures can be taken to reassure them?
- Brand Perception and Trust Levels: Customers need reassurance through proactive messaging and consistent service, especially when the company has suffered reputational damage (e.g., bankruptcy rumors and operational failures).
- Pricing and Product Adjustments: Are customers sensitive to price changes resulting from cost restructuring? Are product offerings aligned with evolving demand trends?

Companies should conduct customer sentiment analysis, direct engagement programs, and loyalty retention initiatives to minimize churn and rebuild customer trust.

Deliverables:

i. The *Stakeholder Impact Matrix* is a mapping framework that categorizes internal and external stakeholders based on their level of influence and impact on the turnaround strategy. This tool helps leadership prioritize key stakeholder relationships and tailor communication strategies accordingly.
ii. The *Engagement Roadmap* is a structured communication and negotiation plan detailing how the company will interact with employees, lenders, investors, suppliers, and customers during the turnaround process. This roadmap includes timelines, messaging strategies, and escalation plans for handling critical stakeholder concerns.

Psychological Dynamics in Phase 1 (Assessment)

Psychologically, companies in distress often exhibit what Kanter called the "death spiral" behaviors: finger-pointing, silo mentality, and passivity. In Phase 1, turnaround CEOs should proactively break the cycle of denial. For instance, holding cross-functional workshops to discuss findings can replace secrecy with dialogue and blame with problem-solving. Identifying and fixing a minor process issue in these early weeks—a small win—can help replace feelings of helplessness with a sense of initiative. According to Kanter's study, effective turnaround CEOs deliberately replace denial with open dialogue, blame with respect, and turf protection with collaboration, thereby setting a new tone. In practice, this might involve sharing difficult truths in an all-hands meeting—for example, emphasizing the new culture of cooperation and positivity ("We have a new culture of collaboration and contribute positively") and reinforcing leadership expectations ("Any leader who doesn't demonstrate this and cascade the culture down will be let go because …"). Afterward, leadership can invite ideas from all levels on ways to conserve cash or improve sales."

People are more likely to open up once they see that leadership confronts reality transparently. Additionally, acknowledge the emotional impact on employees: many will be in shock or fear. Showing empathy (e.g., providing support resources or listening sessions with n-1 and n-2 in private and public) can build the credibility needed to get their buy-in for tough decisions later. In summary, Phase 1 isn't just about gathering data on the business. It's about healing the organization's psyche so everyone is ready to take on the identified challenges.

Final Deliverables:

> **i. Comprehensive Diagnostic Report:** a detailed document covering all assessment areas—strategy, financials, operations, market, organization, stakeholders mapping, etc. This report should coherently illustrate each area's root causes of distress (e.g., "Operational Inefficiency: Plant A operating at 50 percent capacity due to maintenance issues, resulting in high unit costs"). It should incorporate data analysis, for instance, benchmarking the company's KPIs against industry averages to highlight perfor-

mance gaps. The report also identifies immediate risks (such as looming debt repayments or loss of a major customer) that need addressing. Importantly, it doesn't just catalog problems; it provides an analytical bridge to solutions by hinting at potential strategies (e.g., "Excess capacity could be addressed by consolidation or increased sales effort"). Essentially, the diagnostic report is the factual foundation upon which the turnaround plan (Phase 2) will be built. It should be objective and unflinching, as it may be shared with key stakeholders (board members, lenders) to make the case for change.

ii. Benchmarking and Metrics Dashboard: As part of the report or as a standalone deliverable, a benchmarking report compares the company's critical metrics (financial ratios, productivity measures) to those of its peers or industry bests. This could be delivered as a dashboard or scorecard highlighting where the company lags (e.g., industrial leverage is X percent versus industry average Y percent, indicating highly inefficient capitalization and asset utilization).

This quantitative comparison often serves as a wake-up call, quantifying the improvement needed. ("We are 30 percent less efficient than competitors on output per employee.") It also helps set realistic targets for the turnaround (closing half the gap to best-in-class could be an initial goal). Combined with this is a diagnostic scorecard used to track progress in later phases— essentially turning the assessment into measurable KPIs to improve (e.g., raising customer satisfaction from 60 percent to 80 percent, reducing debt-to-equity from 3:1 to 1.5:1, etc.). Delivering this dashboard early signals a data-driven approach to stakeholders and creates accountability in the future.

iii. Executive Summary and Briefing: To facilitate communication, a concise executive summary of Phase 1 findings is prepared for top management, the board, and possibly external stakeholders (like banks or investors). This summary distills the situation into key points, including the main issues, and outlines the broad strokes of the forthcoming plan to address them. It should highlight five to ten priority focus areas that Phase 2 will tackle, e.g., "Improve liquidity—target X million working capital release," "Restructure debt—extend maturities," or "Simplify product portfolio—exit two of five lines."

By providing this bridge to Phase 2, the summary ensures everyone is aligned with what comes next. Typically, this is presented in a meeting to secure buy-in. It's a chance for the CEO or turnaround leader to say, "Here's what we found, and here's where we are going." Clarity at this juncture is crucial to maintain confidence among employees, the board, and creditors that the team has a grip on the problems and that a plan is forming. Many turnarounds falter if stakeholders remain unconvinced after Phase 1; hence, a crisp executive presentation can be as important as the analysis itself in fueling momentum into the Planning Phase.

Phase 2: Planning

Phase 1—Assessment: In Phase 1, we would have conducted a deep diagnostic analysis across corporate strategy, financials, operations, sales, marketing, HR, IT, external market forces, compliance, and stakeholder engagement to pinpoint root causes of distress.

Phase 2—Overview: In Phase 2, the turnaround CEO and team leverage the diagnostic insights to craft a comprehensive turnaround plan that would have gotten buy-in from major stakeholders (e.g., board members, investors, and lenders). This Planning Phase bridges the gap between knowing the problems and taking action. It is about developing strategic initiatives and detailed execution roadmaps to address each major challenge identified in Phase 1. The plan encompasses both short-term fixes (to quickly improve cash flow or stop losses) and long-term restructuring moves (to fundamentally reposition the company for sustainable profitability).

A key aspect of Phase 2 is prioritization—deciding what actions to do first versus later, given limited resources and urgency. There is often a focus on a few "quick wins" that can be executed in the next three to six months to build credibility (for example, divesting a non-core unit to raise cash or launching a marketing campaign to win back key customers). Simultaneously, the plan outlines medium- to long-term transformations, including operational revamps, system upgrades, or growth initiatives. I cannot stress enough the importance of gaining stakeholders' buy-ins since there might be a need for investors' cash injection, change of long-term operational standards, etc.

The Planning Phase should be highly collaborative and communicative. While a core turnaround team might draft the plan, input and alignment from department heads and key stakeholders are crucial to ensure feasibility and buy-in. This is often when tough decisions are crystallized, e.g., how many jobs to cut, which plants to close, and which debts to restructure. Scenario planning is useful: teams may develop best-case, base-case, and worst-case versions of the plan depending on external factors (market recovery, investor support, etc.). By the end of Phase 2, the company should have a formally approved turnaround blueprint with specific initiatives, owners, timelines, and performance targets in place. For instance, when we devised the takeover with the current CEO at AGP Global, we convinced the Philippine government to do the assessment. Once we finished, we had a detailed turnaround plan, incorporating priorities the government valued, like employees' pensions, keeping the company manufacturing in the Philippines, etc. We also detailed the plan to set realistic targets, including achieving a positive net income by year one, increasing operating profits by 10 percent by year two, restructuring the debt, and cutting it in half by year five. Such clarity set the stage for decisive execution in Phase 3.

Developing Turnaround Strategies

Objectives of the Planning Phase: To guide planning, it's essential to set clear goals that the turnaround plan must achieve. These typically include:

> **a. Structured, Cross-Functional Plans:** Ensure the plan covers every critical function (strategy, finance, operations, sales, HR, IT, etc.) in an integrated way. Rather than isolated fixes, Phase 2 produces a coordinated program of initiatives. For example, a cost reduction in operations might need a parallel HR plan for retraining or layoffs and a finance plan for restructuring debt in line with a lower-cost base to convince lenders. The

objective is to avoid siloed plans and execution; instead, create a single roadmap where all moving parts align. Each functional plan should have initiatives that align with the overall turnaround goals. This is critical to gaining company-wide momentum.

Success means that by Phase 3, every department understands its role in the turnaround and how its efforts interact with others (e.g., marketing driving sales volume that feeds into operations planning), illustrating how all departments interconnect—like a human body.

b. Prioritize Quick Wins for Early Cash Flow: Identify two to three initiatives that can deliver tangible improvements within the first few months. Quick wins often involve stopping apparent value leakage or monetizing assets. Examples include selling excess inventory or a redundant asset, implementing a price increase or promotion to boost revenue, aggressively collecting overdue payments, or eliminating an unnecessary management layer. These moves can generate positive cash flow or cost savings quickly. The reasons quick wins are critical are psychological and financial: they build confidence in the turnaround (stakeholders see progress), and they may fund longer-term investments.

One impactful, quick win I helped implement at a Saudi AC manufacturing company involved improving compressor fault detection. Initially, faults were captured during performance testing at a 5 percent failure rate. We changed the testing to happen at the component assembly line, which led to several significant improvements:

- Reduced fault rates
- Lower bottleneck time in performance testing
- Reduced cost by 50 percent
- Decreased assembly-to-market time by 25 percent

When planning, it's crucial to ensure that opportunities like this are not overlooked in favor of big strategic moves. Dedicate a section of the plan to "Quick Wins in the Next 100 Days" and assign owners to them.

c. Long-Term Transformation Goals: While pursuing quick wins, long-term targets (usually one to three years out) that define success for the turnaround must also be set. These could be financial (e.g., achieving a 15 percent EBITDA margin or reaching revenue of $X by year three), operational (e.g., industry-leading quality or delivery times), or strategic (e.g., entering two new markets or shifting the business model to a subscription-based one). These goals should align with industry benchmarks or investor expectations for a healthy company in that sector. For instance, if peers have a debt-to-equity ratio of 1:1, a long-term goal might be to deleverage to that level. If top competitors grow at 10 percent annually, a goal might be to regain comparable growth. Setting these targets gives the organization a north star—it's not just about surviving but thriving. The plan then details how to get there. The presence of long-term goals also helps with stakeholder management: creditors and shareholders are more likely to support painful changes if they see the promised land of improved performance and value creation.

d. Clear Accountability and Milestones: A plan is only as good as its execution. Therefore, assign a responsible owner (person or team) to define key milestones and KPIs for each initiative and articulate them clearly. For example, if one initiative is to "reduce overhead costs by 20 percent," the plan should specify which executive sponsor will lead this effort and include interim checkpoints (10 percent reduction in 3 months, 20 percent by 9 months). Building a timeline (often with 3, 9, 12, and 18-month milestones) helps sequence actions: some steps (like renegotiating leases) might happen in year 2 if the immediate focus is elsewhere. Laying this out turns the strategy into a project plan that can be monitored.

Milestones also create accountability moments, e.g., a 6-month review to check if Phase 3 execution is on track. A CEO should appoint a direct report to serve as a transformative officer (or PMO, depending on naming conventions and avoiding duplication of titles to avoid confusion) under their office, often responsible for tracking all these milestones at this stage. The objective is that everyone knows who is responsible for what by when, and leaves no ambiguity as the organization moves to execution.

e. Stakeholder Alignment: Before finalizing, ensure key stakeholders review and accept the plan. Internally, this means the senior leadership

Phase 2: Planning

team, influential managers, or employee representatives. Externally, it might include major shareholders, creditors (such as banks and sukuk holders), the board of directors, and possibly regulators (if in a regulated industry). Aligning stakeholders may involve tough negotiations, such as convincing creditors to extend loans as the plan shows eventual recovery. During planning, hold frequent update meetings or workshops with these stakeholders to incorporate their feedback and secure buy-ins. A well-aligned plan might secure commitments, such as new funding from investors or temporary concessions (such as landlords reducing rent or suppliers adjusting terms) because stakeholders see a credible path forward. Essentially, by the end of Phase 2, the turnaround plan should be well-crafted and have the necessary support needed for execution, avoiding battles in Phase 3 that could derail progress.

Deliverables:

- **Strategic Turnaround Framework**: a structured approach outlining the key pillars of the turnaround, including financial stabilization, operational efficiency, revenue growth, and organizational realignment
- **Scenario Planning & Risk Mitigation Strategy**: a detailed plan assessing best-case, base-case, and worst-case scenarios, with contingency actions to mitigate financial, operational, and stakeholder risks
- **Value Creation Playbook**: a roadmap identifying high-impact initiatives to generate measurable financial and operational improvements, ensuring a structured execution plan with clear ROI expectations

Corporate Strategy and Business Model Realignment

In this sub-section of planning, the team addresses **high-level strategic changes** needed for the company's future viability:

    a. Define Clear Turnaround Objectives: Start by translating the broad goals into specific targets for the company's strategy. For example, set short-term (0–6 months) objectives focused on stabilization, such as "Restore monthly cash breakeven within 3 months," and medium to long-term (3–18+ months) objectives aimed at growth or competitive repositioning. These objectives should cover multiple dimensions, including revenue growth, cost reduction, operational efficiency, and organizational and cultural changes. The team ensures balance by categorizing objectives (e.g., revenue initiatives, cost initiatives, and process improvements).

b. Actionable Strategy: For each objective, identify at a high level the strategic moves required to achieve it. If a goal is revenue growth, is it achieved by entering a new market, launching new products, or increasing share in current segments? If cost reduction is the goal, is it downsizing, outsourcing, or process innovation? The output here is essentially a *strategy blueprint* that may say, "Within two years, exit unprofitable markets, focus on our core region, achieve 20 percent cost reduction, and invest in a digital sales channel to drive new growth." Such clarity will direct the more detailed plans to other sections (operations, marketing, etc.).

Additionally, realign the business model if needed. Perhaps the assessment determined that the current model (e.g., selling capital equipment one-off) is less viable, and a new model (e.g., leasing with service contracts) is needed for steady revenue. Planning would outline this shift and prepare the organization to pilot or implement it. Essentially, this step sets the *strategic backbone* of the turnaround plan.

c. Portfolio Rationalization and Core Focus: Determine which parts of the business to *keep, fix,* or *divest*. Many troubled companies suffer from pursuing too many initiatives or holding onto legacy businesses that no longer align with their future. Using data from Phase 1, identify non-core or underperforming business lines, brands, or assets. Develop criteria (e.g., negative profit, no strategic synergy, requiring excessive capital, or increasing industrial leverage) to mark these for exit. Concurrently, pinpoint the core high-potential areas that merit more focus and investment. Planning should outline the divestiture strategy for each item marked as non-core: Will it be an outright sale, wind-down, or spin-off? What timeline and steps are involved (hire a broker, find buyers, etc.)?

Estimating the cash that could be raised or costs saved by divesting is indispensable and must be fed into the financial plan. For the core businesses, strategy realignment means outlining how to *double down* on them —perhaps reallocating capital to a star product line or refocusing R&D on the most promising technology. For example, at AGP, we decided to drop all services unrelated to oil refineries, moved all manpower to its own division, and bring in procurement and design in-house, essentially becoming a vertically integrated EPC contractor for oil refineries, reducing the time it used to take to develop an oil refinery from two years to nine months. The plan should outline which businesses or assets will be sold or closed (and by when) and how the company will reallocate resources to the remaining core operations to drive growth and profitability.

Deliverables:

- **Executive Strategy Roadmap with 3, 9, and 18-Month Milestones**: a phased plan mapping out key strategic initiatives, ensuring alignment between short-term stabilization and long-term transformation objectives.
- **Product/Market Profitability Analysis and Business Prioritization Matrix**: a data-driven evaluation of product lines, customer segments, and markets to determine which should be scaled, optimized, or divested.
- **Premortem Risk Report and Assessment**: an analysis identifying potential failure points in the turnaround plan, with preemptive mitigation strategies to ensure resilience during execution (not your regular risk registrar).

Financial Restructuring and Capital Optimization

A critical part of planning is addressing the *financial structure*, ensuring the company's capital and costs align with its turnaround needs:

    a. **Liquidity and Working Capital Management Plan:** Building on

Phase 1's findings, create a plan to ensure the company has enough cash through the turnaround.

b. Short-Term (0–3 months): Maximize liquidity immediately. This includes continuing Phase 1 measures, such as tight spending controls and aggressive working capital tactics.

c. Plan specifics include:

- Decide how to enforce ongoing expense discipline (e.g., require CEO approval for any spend above a threshold).
- Set targets for reducing receivable days and inventory levels (maybe adopting "Just-in-Time" for inventory or offering early pay incentives to customers)
- Detail external financing arrangements (e.g., a credit line usage schedule).

d. Medium-term (3–6 months): Plan for more structural improvements, such as implementing a new cash management system or renegotiating payment terms with suppliers to standardize at 60 days. Additionally, consider *asset-based loans* or *sale-leaseback transactions* on idle assets to unlock the cash value needed.

e. Long-term (6–24 months): Integrate sustained working capital improvements, such as automated credit control systems, vendor-managed inventory, etc., so that once the company recovers, it operates on a leaner working capital model. An example could be centralizing procurement to get bulk discounts (improving cash by paying less) while using surplus cash later to negotiate early-pay discounts from vendors (saving cost). The plan should project a *cash flow forecast* that reflects these actions, demonstrating the company's ability to meet its obligations and invest as needed over the turnaround period.

f. Debt Restructuring Strategy: If the company is over-indebted or facing tight covenants, the plan must outline how to restructure liabilities. This could involve negotiations with lenders to extend maturities, reduce interest rates, or obtain covenant waivers until performance improves. Sometimes, a more drastic approach may be required, such as a debt-for-equity swap. If an agreement isn't possible, another option is to approach the Ministry of Commerce or the Ministry of Finance for supervised reorganization. However, this is typically a last resort due to its complexity, impact, and the introduction of additional complex stakeholders. A good example is Jabal Omar, where the Ministry of Finance's involvement complicated negotiations with banks, ultimately delaying repayment by years.

Planning should identify which debt facilities are problematic (those with upcoming maturity or currently in default) and prioritize them for restructuring discussions. Prepare a creditor presentation using the turnaround plan to convince them that extending support now will yield better recovery later (e.g., show projections that debt ratios will improve significantly by year two if the plan succeeds). Also, explore refinancing options: can new investors or funds replace some debt with equity or more patient capital? A notable case is LyondellBasell, a petrochemical firm that used Chapter 11 bankruptcy to eliminate about $20 billion in debt and emerge with a healthier balance sheet (economictimes.indiatimes.com). The planning involved renegotiating with dozens of creditors and acquiring new equity backers. Even outside of bankruptcy, the turnaround plan should earmark specific assets for sale to pay down debt and model the impact on interest costs. The goal is to create a *sustainable capital structure* (debt levels that the recovered business can service comfortably). KPIs might include target debt-to-equity or interest coverage ratios by specific dates.

g. Capital Expenditure and Investment Prioritization: In a state of distress or turnaround, capital is relatively scarce. However, some investment might be needed to fix issues (e.g., upgrading an IT system, performing deferred maintenance, or developing a critical new product). The plan should establish a *capital allocation strategy*: what minimal but vital capital expenditures (capex) are required during the turnaround, and how will they be funded? Rank projects by necessity and return on investment. For instance, if a production line is at risk of failing without new parts, that capex is nonnegotiable. However, an expansion to a new office is likely deferrable. If cash allows, the plan might include a small "opportunistic investment" budget to seize potential strategic opportunities (i.e., when a competitor's asset becomes available at a discounted price). Ensure that all planned investments tie back to the turnaround's objectives (there should be no "nice to haves," only "must haves").

Additionally, include a *contingency reserve* in the financial plan—a cushion for unexpected costs, which often occur in turnarounds. This shows prudence to stakeholders. Practically, Phase 2 would result in a revised *budget and cash flow forecast* for the next one to two years, incorporating cost cuts and investments, demonstrating that with these moves, the company can operate within its means and generate positive cash flow.

Deliverables:

- **Liquidity and Working Capital Action Plan**: a short-term financial strategy focused on improving cash flow through cost reductions, supplier renegotiations, and working capital efficiencies
- **Debt Restructuring Proposal**: a structured framework for renegotiating debt terms, including refinancing options, payment deferrals, or alternative capital sources to ensure financial stability
- **Budget Optimization Framework**: a zero-based budgeting approach ensuring all expenditures are justified, prioritizing high-ROI investments while eliminating non-essential costs.

Operational Improvement Roadmaps

Phase 2 Planning must detail how to fix and optimize the business operations. This is where Lean principles and process reengineering plans come in:

a. Efficiency Initiatives: Based on Phase 1's operational findings, design specific initiatives to improve efficiency. For a manufacturing firm, this could mean launching a *Lean Transformation Program*, which involves implementing 5S in plants, initiating Kaizen projects on the biggest bottlenecks, and reducing changeover times, among other measures. Quantify the goals (e.g., improve overall equipment effectiveness from 60 percent to 80 percent within nine months, reduce scrap rate by half) and reduce incidents to zero.

For a service organization, efficiency might involve *process redesign* or *automation*. For instance, a bank might plan to automate loan processing to cut turnaround time from five days to one day. These initiatives should be mapped facility by facility or process by process. Include any technology enablement (like installing IoT sensors for predictive maintenance as part of Industry 4.0 adoption to plan maintenance during downtime, etc). The plan should outline required investments and expected savings for each initiative. Phase 2 would specify the Six Sigma projects, the training needed, and the timeline to achieve them. Each initiative gets an owner (operations manager or team) and a timeline (some quick hits in one to three months, others in nine-plus months if they require capital).

b. Footprint and Capacity Optimization: If the company has multiple plants, warehouses, or service centers, planning might involve *consolidation or expansion* strategies. For example, decide whether to close an underutilized plant and redistribute production to other sites (to achieve economies of scale and higher utilization). Alternatively, if demand is expected to grow, plan to ramp up capacity in a cost-effective way. This includes evaluating outsourcing versus insourcing—maybe outsourcing non-core manufacturing to a third party to save costs while focusing internal capacity on high-margin products. Each such move in the plan should have a justification (e.g., closing Plant X will save $Y per year, and we have enough capacity at Plant Y to absorb volume, raising its utilization from 60 percent to 85 percent). In service industries, this could mean consolidating offices, moving to a cheaper location, or online service delivery.

Also, plan the logistics/supply chain optimization, e.g., reduce the number of distribution centers if that cuts costs without hurting service, or renegotiate 3PL contracts. Ensure the plan covers the one-time expenses, such as severance for a plant closure or contract termination fees, and includes them in the financial section. The expected outcome (to be achieved in Phase 3) would be a leaner operation footprint that matches the business size and strategy, directly contributing to cost reduction goals.

c. Quality and Customer Service Improvements: Turnarounds aren't just about cutting. Improving quality and service is often necessary to win back customers and drive revenue. If Phase 1 showed customer dissatisfaction or high return rates, Phase 2 should include a plan to address these. For manufacturing, consider implementing *Total Quality Management* or obtaining critical certifications (e.g., ISO 9001) to signal a renewed quality focus with a carefully crafted communication strategy to gain trust. Plan a *customer experience initiative* for services, such as training staff to deliver better service, introducing a customer feedback loop, or investing in CRM systems to provide personalized service. One actionable item could be setting up real-time customer satisfaction dashboards and response teams similar to what Emirates does on its flights. The plan might target specific metrics, such as improving the Net Promoter Score (NPS) from X to Y or increasing on-time delivery from A percent to B percent. Including these in the plan ensures the turnaround is not solely inward-focused but also rebuilds market trust and loyalty. This, in turn, supports the revenue side of the turnaround—happy customers lead to repeat business and positive word of mouth, fueling growth in Phase 4.

Deliverables:

- **Operations Dashboard Tracking Efficiency Gains:** a real-time tracking system measuring cost reductions, productivity improvements, and operational KPIs to monitor turnaround progress
- **Supplier Renegotiation Plan and Cost Reduction Analysis:** a detailed strategy for lowering procurement costs, optimizing vendor contracts, and improving supply chain efficiency
- **Manufacturing Process Improvement Roadmap:** a structured framework for deploying lean manufacturing, automation, and process optimizations to reduce waste, cycle times, and defects

Sales and Marketing Turnaround Strategy

a. Market Positioning and Brand Rejuvenation

Conduct Market Research to Identify Growth Segments

A company undergoing a turnaround must reassess its market dynamics to identify profitable growth segments and areas of competitive advantage. A detailed market research process should:

i. **Analyze consumer behavior shifts**: Are customers demanding more digital experiences, environmentally friendly products, or price-conscious alternatives?
ii. **Assess emerging trends**: Are AI-driven personalization, automation, or direct-to-consumer models disrupting traditional business models?
iii. **Identify underserved or high-margin niches:** Focusing on profitable, high-growth customer segments in a turnaround ensures efficient resource allocation.

For instance, if a manufacturing firm realizes that smaller batch, customized production is more profitable than high-volume, low-margin production, repositioning its offerings accordingly can create a competitive edge. B2B companies should assess growing vertical markets, while retailers should explore digital engagement opportunities (e.g., subscription models or influencer-driven sales).

Reposition Brand Messaging to Align with Evolving Customer Needs

A distressed company often suffers from negative brand perception due to operational challenges, poor customer service, or declining product quality. To restore trust and relevance, it must refine its brand positioning strategy by:

i. **Clarifying the Unique Selling Proposition (USP)**: What differentiates the company in the current market? If competitors focus on cost-cutting, repositioning around superior service or product innovation can be an effective strategy.
   i. **Addressing Reputation Damage**: If the company has faced public trust issues, targeted messaging through crisis communication, PR campaigns, and customer engagement initiatives is critical.

ii. **Leveraging New Distribution Channels**: If the brand was primarily brick-and-mortar, shifting toward e-commerce and social commerce (e.g., influencer marketing, shoppable content) may be necessary to regain lost market share.

For example, a legacy retail brand might shift from a traditional store-first positioning to a "digital-first, experience-driven" brand identity, appealing to younger, tech-savvy consumers.

b. Salesforce and Revenue Optimization Plan

Introducing Commission-Based Incentives to Drive Performance

In a turnaround, sales productivity is paramount. If the sales team lacks motivation or alignment with turnaround goals, restructuring compensation models can boost performance. Key tactics include:

i. **Performance-Based Commission Structures:** Shifting from flat salaries to tiered commission models rewards high performers and drives urgency in closing deals.
   i. **Strategic Sales KPIs:** Compensation should align with high-value outcomes, such as:
      1. Closing larger contracts (instead of volume-based selling)
      2. Retaining existing customers (bonus for renewal rates)
      3. Expanding share-of-wallet (incentives for cross-selling and upselling)
      4. Increase the customer-lifetime-value focus
      5. Rewarding collaboration efforts with higher commissions and recognition
      6. Customer satisfaction rating
   ii. **Gamification and Real-Time Dashboards:** Incorporating leaderboards, recognition programs, and AI-driven performance analytics can motivate sales teams and improve accountability.

For instance, SaaS companies often use performance-based commissions with accelerators for multi-year contracts, ensuring both immediate cash flow and long-term revenue stability. Others, such as new healthcare trends, are increasing the lifetime value of a patient. For example, when a young patient comes in, the doctor no longer focuses on generating income from the patient through meaningless testing and unnecessary medicine, justified by specific protocols to avoid regulatory fines and ethical dilemmas. Instead, the hospital or clinic rewards the doctor for creating long-term patient relationships. These rewards are based on repeated visits, frequent patient contact, satisfaction levels, and the patient's rating of the doctor and staff.

Improve Customer Segmentation and Targeting to Focus on the Lifetime Value of Clients

A distressed company must prioritize customer segments that generate the highest profit and increase lifetime value. The turnaround strategy should:

ii. **Analyze historical purchase data:** Which customers generate high margins but are underserved?
   i. **Develop AI-driven segmentation models:** Machine learning can cluster customers based on their propensity to buy, churn risk, and cross-sell potential.
   ii. **Personalize marketing and sales approaches:** Using data-driven recommendations, targeted offers, relationship-building strategies, empowering salespeople, and AI-powered dynamic pricing improves conversion rates.

For example, an industrial manufacturer might discover that repeat buyers contribute 80 percent of revenue, leading to a strategy shift and organizational change from acquiring new clients to upselling existing ones through service contracts.

Expand Digital Sales Channels

Companies must diversify revenue streams by investing in high-ROI digital channels. Key areas to explore include:

i. **E-commerce Enablement:** If the company sells physical

products, a direct-to-consumer (DTC) model or marketplace partnerships (Amazon, Shopify, etc.) can drive higher margins.
  ii. **Social Selling and Influencer Marketing:** Leveraging TikTok, Instagram Shopping, and LinkedIn Sales Navigator allows companies to capture digital-first audiences.
  iii. **AI-Driven Conversational Sales:** Chatbots and AI-powered assistants can automate lead qualification, follow-ups, and upselling in real time. However, they should be carefully deployed to avoid creating additional layers of the customer journey.

For example, a B2B logistics firm could expand by adding self-service digital procurement portals, reducing sales friction, and improving order efficiency. Another example is an airline company with low satisfaction ratings from clients and employees due to poor service quality and scheduling management for pilots and staff alike. Instead of using AI to improve scheduling and employee satisfaction to drive quality, the company prioritizes adding an AI chatbot—an additional step in connecting customers with a human agent.

c. Customer Retention and Pricing Strategy

Reduce Churn by Enhancing Loyalty Programs

Retaining existing customers is five times cheaper than acquiring new ones, making churn reduction a top priority in a turnaround. Companies should:

- **Analyze churn drivers:** Are customers leaving due to price sensitivity, poor service, or product issues? AI-driven churn analytics can provide insights.
- **Launch customer engagement initiatives:** Offering exclusive benefits, early-access promotions, and personalized experiences fosters loyalty.
- **Incentivize long-term commitments:** Subscription-based discounts, extended warranties, or bundled service plans improve retention.

For instance, Saudi Telecom Company often introduces contract buyouts and retention-focused perks (such as priority customers like the Tamyouz Program) to prevent churn.

Implement Dynamic Pricing Models to Increase Profit Margins

In distressed scenarios, rigid pricing structures often lead to revenue leakage. AI-powered dynamic pricing algorithms can optimize margins by:

- **Analyzing Demand Fluctuations:** Adjusting prices based on real-time market conditions, inventory levels, and customer behavior ensures competitiveness.
- **Segmenting Pricing by Lifetime Value:** VIP customers can be offered premium pricing bundles, while price-sensitive segments can receive discounted entry-level offers.
- **Competitive Intelligence Adjustments:** Tracking rival pricing models and promotional strategies enables agile decision-making.

For example, airlines use AI-driven pricing to adjust fares dynamically, maximizing revenue per seat while remaining competitive. F&B companies in the UAE (now starting in Saudi Arabia) use service providers like BurgerIndex to monitor competitors' pricing in promoting and doing instant matching.

Bundle Products/Services to Drive Upselling and Cross-Selling

Bundling increases customer lifetime value while reducing customer acquisition costs. Strategies include:

- **Product Bundling:** Offering complementary products together at a discounted rate encourages larger transactions.
- **Service-Based Upselling:** Subscription-based companies can offer premium tiers or value-added services (e.g., VIP support, faster delivery).
- **AI-Powered Recommendation Engines:** Retailers can leverage AI to automate personalized bundling, improving cross-sell rates.

For instance, software companies often bundle security features with core platforms, increasing retention while enhancing customer stickiness.

Deliverables:

- **Market Expansion and Pricing Strategy Document:** a comprehensive plan outlining new market opportunities, repositioning strategies, and AI-driven pricing models to optimize margins
- **CRM and Salesforce Performance Improvement Plan:** a strategic blueprint for salesforce restructuring, customer segmentation enhancements, and incentive-based commission structures to accelerate revenue recovery

Organization and Workforce Plan (Human Capital)

No turnaround can succeed without addressing the *people dimension*. Phase 2 must devise a plan for the organization's structure, talent, and culture:

a. Workforce Restructuring and Talent Deployment: Based on the new strategy operational plan and stakeholder mapping, determine the implications for headcount and skills. Often, distress forces difficult choices, such as layoffs or furloughs, to cut costs. The plan should identify areas where redundancies exist, e.g., where layers of management can be removed to flatten the organization or low-performing business units whose staff may be exited or redeployed. Clearly outline the scale of workforce reduction (e.g., "Reduce workforce by 15 percent, 100 positions, over the next 6 months") and the associated process (voluntary separation programs, performance-based cuts, etc.). It is just as important to identify *critical talent gaps* for the turnaround: perhaps (and common in Saudi Arabia), a company lacks a Chief Marketing Officer experienced in digital sales or needs more salespeople in a region targeted for growth. Plan to recruit or internally promote for these roles quickly, so leadership is in place for Phase 3. Also include a *change management team or chief transformation officer* role (this can also be a director in the CEO's office, depending on the company and its mandate), if not already appointed, to drive execution.

Essentially, redesign the organizational chart to fit the future. This could involve consolidating divisions, creating new teams (like a Project Management Office reporting to the CEO to track initiatives), and eliminating silos. One actionable example was at Duet in India. We wanted to eliminate the dependency on Marriott, so we established a division dedicated to OTA services that we can handle directly. The plan should schedule these organizational changes (e.g., announce new organizational structure by month 3, complete layoffs by month 4, and hire key positions by month 6). This blueprint allows the Phase 3 implementation of workforce changes to be swift and less chaotic.

b. Leadership and Governance Initiatives: If the company's leadership was part of the problem (common in turnaround-required companies), Phase 2 might involve changes at the top. This could include succession plans or replacements for certain executives. For instance, the plan might note to "bring in a turnaround-experienced CFO" or "transition founder-CEO" to a chairman role and recruit a "new CEO with restructuring experience." Additionally, strengthen governance: I would like to add various key committees to increase transparency and accountability and improve governance. For example, when hiring, I want to establish a "Hiring Committee" and a "Culture Committee." I envision hiring as a five-step process, ensuring the right "who" is employed. (I will expand on this later.)

Perhaps a temporary turnaround committee should be formed on the board to provide more frequent oversight during the recovery period. (Note: An ideal number of internal committees is four to five. An additional three board committees would be the best practice and should not exceed eight or nine total committees at the company executive and board level.) Ensure the plan addresses any *cultural leadership issues* identified in Phase 1, such as whether decision-making was too centralized or lacked accountability. Introduce new governance mechanisms, such as weekly executive committee meetings to review turnaround progress or KPI dashboards to which leaders must respond. Also, plan how to *communicate the new vision* from leadership to the broader organization. A leadership roadshow and/or town-halls might be scheduled to rally the troops once the plan is in place. Essentially, this part of the plan covers the "soft" infrastructure that will drive the hard results: ensuring the right people are in the right roles and that leadership has the forums and metrics to guide the company out of trouble. Top-tier firms often advise setting up a *Transformation Office* under the CEO to coordinate all this, so expect the plan to formalize that structure and its responsibilities.

c. Incentives and Change Enablers: Aligning incentives with turnaround goals is a powerful tool that brings together key elements around the turnaround strategy. The plan should consider modifications to *compensation structures*. For example, to motivate employees, introduce performance-based bonuses tied to turnaround KPIs (cash flow targets, cost savings achieved, etc.). Equity grants or upside sharing for key managers can encourage them to stay and push for a successful outcome (especially if the current stock value is depressed). Offering stock that could multiply in value if the turnaround succeeds can be a strong motivator. Training and development also come into play: identify whether employees need new skills to execute the plan (e.g., training on leveraging an AI model for manufacturing or Lean training for supervisors in manufacturing). Include a training schedule and budget in the plan to equip the team.

Additionally, plan cultural interventions: launch an internal communications strategy to reinforce the *urgency for change* and then progressively celebrate small successes to shift mindsets from pessimism to optimism. My favorite is forming multiple cross-departmental teams to propose solutions and solve turnaround problems, implementing town hall meetings, internal newsletters, anonymous emails to the CEO to cut through information gates, and recognition programs to keep morale and engagement high through the tough times. For example, after major milestones (like hitting a cost-cut target), the CEO might publicly recognize the teams involved—the plan should schedule such morale-boosting actions. By baking in these change management tactics, Phase 2 ensures that when execution begins, the organization's *human element is prepared and incentivized* to drive the turnaround, not resist it.

Deliverables:

- **Revised Leadership Structure and Accountability Framework**: This document outlines new executive responsibilities, leadership changes, and governance enhancements to ensure transparent decision-making and execution discipline. It formalizes reporting lines and key performance metrics and introduces new governance committees, including turnaround oversight committees, a Culture Committee, and executive transformation offices.
- **Employee Engagement and Motivation Plan**: A strategic roadmap detailing incentive structures, cultural change initiatives, and communication strategies to boost employee morale during the turnaround. It includes performance-based compensation adjustments, training schedules for critical skills development, and internal communication channels (e.g., town halls, newsletters, anonymous feedback mechanisms) to drive engagement and transparency.

Digital Transformation and IT Optimization

a. **IT Cost Rationalization**

Identifying Non-Essential IT Spending and Eliminating Redundancies

One of the quickest ways to improve financial stability in a turnaround is to identify nonessential IT expenses that do not contribute to core business objectives. Companies often accumulate legacy software, unused licenses, and redundant cloud services, leading to unnecessary overhead.

A complete IT cost audit should categorize expenditures into:

i. **Critical IT Functions:** directly impacting business continuity (e.g., ERP, cybersecurity tools)
ii. **Efficiency-Enhancing Systems:** productivity tools, automation, and customer service technologies

iii. **Nonessential or Redundant Tools:** legacy software that overlaps with modern solutions, underutilized SaaS subscriptions, hardware that can be sold, or unnecessary storage costs

By eliminating non-strategic IT expenses and consolidating overlapping functionalities, businesses can improve cost efficiency while redirecting resources toward digital transformation initiatives.

Optimizing Software Licensing Agreements

Companies often overpay for IT services due to poor software license management. A key part of cost optimization is renegotiating software agreements, rightsizing usage, outsourcing all licensing needs if applicable, and leveraging volume discounts where possible.

Key actions include:

i. License Usage Review: Identify unused or underutilized software licenses. If only 50 percent of CRM licenses are actively used, the company is overpaying for dormant seats.
ii. Cloud and SaaS Spending Optimization: Companies with multiple SaaS subscriptions should bundle vendor contracts to receive discounts.
iii. Vendor Renegotiations: During financial distress, vendors may be willing to extend payment terms or offer cost reductions to maintain long-term relationships.

A contract optimization strategy ensures that IT spending aligns with operational priorities and maximizes cost-saving opportunities.

a. Automation and AI Integration

Using RPA (Robotic Process Automation) for Back-Office Efficiency

RPA (Robotic Process Automation) is a cost-effective way to improve turnaround execution without increasing headcount. RPA uses software bots to automate repetitive, rule-based tasks, reducing errors and boosting efficiency.

Key areas for RPA adoption:

  i. **Finance and Accounting:** automating invoice processing, payroll, and financial reconciliations
  ii. **Customer and/or Employee Support:** using AI chatbots to handle FAQs, reducing call center and HR workloads
  iii. **Supply Chain and Inventory Management:** automating order processing, tracking, and restocking triggers

By eliminating manual workflows, companies reduce operational costs, enhance accuracy, and free up employees to focus on strategic tasks. That said, this also needs to be carefully planned, ideally starting with automating the most basic and repetitive tasks internally before moving on to automation for customers. Having a ready feedback loop to make quick improvements and/or decisions on automation. The turnaround strategy should prioritize RPA in departments with high manual workloads for immediate efficiency gains.

Introducing AI-Driven Predictive Analytics for Decision-Making

Predictive analytics empower decision-makers using AI to forecast financial performance, market trends, and operational risks based on historical data.

Key AI applications in turnarounds include:

  i. **Financial Forecasting:** AI-driven models analyze historical financials, economic trends and correlations, and customer behavior to project future revenue streams and dependencies.
  ii. **Customer Insights and Retention Models:** AI predicts churn risks, helping sales teams proactively engage at-risk customers by analyzing customer behavior and competitors' behavior.
  iii. **Supply Chain Optimization:** AI-powered demand forecasting ensures optimal inventory levels and reduces excess costs.

Integrating predictive analytics into decision-making reduces uncertainty, improves resource allocation, and guides turnaround priorities with data-driven insights.

b. Cybersecurity and Compliance Enhancement

Cyber Risk Assessments to Prevent Security Breaches

Cybersecurity is often deprioritized during financial distress, leaving companies vulnerable to data breaches and operational disruptions. A turnaround should prioritize cybersecurity risk assessments to identify critical vulnerabilities and prevent catastrophic losses.

Key cyber risk areas to evaluate:

i. **Access Control and Credential Management:** Ensure multi-factor authentication (MFA) and eliminate excessive admin privileges.
ii. **Threat Intelligence and Monitoring:** Deploy AI-driven anomaly detection for real-time cyber threat identification.
iii. **Data Backup and Recovery Plans:** Ensure disaster recovery mechanisms are in place to prevent data loss from, for example, ransomware attacks.

A proactive cybersecurity approach ensures that digital threats do not disrupt turnaround efforts and protect critical data assets. Ensure IT systems comply with data laws (such as PDPL, CMA, and others).

Ensuring IT Compliance with Data Laws

Data privacy compliance is essential for avoiding regulatory fines and maintaining customer trust. Companies must ensure that their IT systems adhere to *industry-specific laws* such as:

i. **Saudi PDPL (Personal Data Protection Law):** This law mandates strict regulations for data collection, processing, and storage, requiring businesses to obtain explicit consent before processing personal data.
ii. **NCA Essential Cybersecurity Controls (ECC-1:2018):** These establish cybersecurity baseline controls to prevent data breaches, requiring real-time monitoring, access control policies, and incident response frameworks.

iii. **SAMA Cybersecurity Framework** (for financial institutions): Banks and fintech companies must comply with the Saudi Central Bank's security controls, ensuring encryption of sensitive transactions and fraud detection mechanisms.

Failure to maintain compliance can damage the brand and lead to legal penalties—a risk that turnaround companies cannot afford to take. A comprehensive IT compliance audit ensures regulatory alignment and risk mitigation.

Deliverables:

- **IT Transformation Roadmap:** a structured step-by-step plan detailing how IT cost optimizations, automation, AI integration, and security improvements will be implemented.
- **Cost-benefit Analysis of Digital Investments:** a financial breakdown of IT spending versus expected efficiency gains, ensuring technology investments align with business priorities.

Stakeholder Communication and Change Management

a. **Lender and Investor Engagement Plan**

Developing a Turnaround Narrative to Rebuild Market Confidence

A successful turnaround hinges on stakeholder confidence. Investors and lenders must see a clear, actionable plan that outlines:

i. Why did the company struggle (root causes)?
ii. What is changing (corrective measures)?
iii. How will financial recovery be achieved?

Key Communication Strategies:

i. **Investor Presentations:** Provide monthly financial updates that outline the progress of cost reductions, revenue growth, and restructuring efforts.

ii. **Debt Restructuring Discussions:** Present a realistic repayment plan and demonstrate operational improvements.
iii. **Strategic Partnerships:** Investors often prefer turnaround plans with new growth strategies (e.g., partnerships, acquisitions).

By demonstrating transparency, companies increase investor buy-in, improving the likelihood of continued funding or extended loan terms.

Providing Monthly Financial and Operational Updates

Stakeholders require real-time visibility into turnaround progress. A structured reporting cadence ensures:

i. **Financial Recovery Milestones:** This may include liquidity updates, debt reduction tracking, and revenue improvements.
ii. **Operational KPIs:** These reflect workforce productivity, cost savings, and progress in digital transformation.
iii. **Market and Competitive Positioning:** Investor confidence increases when management proactively shares industry positioning updates.

Companies should adopt AI-powered dashboards for real-time reporting to ensure transparency and reduce financial ambiguity.

b. **Customer and Supplier Engagement Strategy**

Addressing Concerns About Business Continuity

Customers and suppliers often fear instability in distressed businesses. To maintain trust:

i. **Customer Outreach Campaigns:** Use proactive reassurance via direct communication, retention incentives, and service guarantees.
ii. **Supplier Negotiations:** Securing extended payment terms and volume-based discounts ensures continued supply chain stability. This can be achieved through communication and engaging them in the turnaround plan when it is viable and sensible.

Phase 2: Planning

A structured communication roadmap reassures both parties that turnaround strategies support long-term sustainability.

Offering Incentives for Long-Term Commitments

Customer and supplier retention is critical during a turnaround. Companies can deploy:

 i. **Volume Discount Agreements:** Encourage bulk orders to improve short-term cash flow.
 ii. **Exclusive Partnership Incentives:** Offer priority servicing, more extended warranties, or bundled services to incentivize retention.
 iii. **Flexible Contract Terms:** Reassure customers and suppliers with performance-based renewal options to ensure long-term stability.

Strategic incentives create loyalty, improving cash flow stability.

   c. **Internal Employee Communication Plan**

Regular Town Halls to Align Employees with Turnaround Goals

Transparency is essential in gaining employee buy-in. Regular town halls, leadership Q&A sessions, and anonymous reporting channels ensure:

 i. Clarity on turnaround progress
 ii. Reassurance regarding layoffs or structural changes
 iii. Motivation through performance-based recognition
 iv. Reduce uncertainty and anxiety, and bring fairness and transparency during turnaround

A well-informed workforce is more engaged, productive, and aligned with leadership vision.

Deliverables:

- **Communication Strategy**: a detailed plan with a pulse check on stakeholders outlining how investors, customers, and employees

will be reassured throughout the turnaround, key messaging, and delivery plans
- **Transparent Stakeholder Reporting Structure**: a monthly reporting framework ensures consistent financial and operational updates to lenders, investors, and employees

Psychological Considerations in Phase 2 (Planning)

During the Planning Phase, managing the psychology of stakeholders is just as crucial as the technical planning. This is the phase where the reality of change starts to sink in across the organization—rumors may swirl about layoffs or closures as plans are formulated. Leadership should be *proactive in communication* to prevent paralysis or panic. One of the things I like to do in any company is to share a high-level vision early ("We're crafting a plan to secure our future, and it will involve tough decisions but also new opportunities") to give employees a sense of direction, even if all details aren't public yet. This openness can reduce the anxiety that comes with uncertainty.

It's also essential to involve mid-level managers in the planning process (at least in their area of expertise). Psychologically, people tend to support what they help create. I like to have one-on-one meetings with all n-1 and n-2 leaders to hear them out and identify those who can contribute and those who are undecided. By soliciting input, such as "How can your department reduce costs by 10 percent without harming service?", the turnaround CEO gets ground-level insights while *fostering ownership* of the plan among those who will implement it. This counters the common "us versus them" mentality that can arise if plans are perceived as top-down edicts.

From a change management theory perspective, create a sense of urgency (most in a turnaround already feel this) and *build a coalition* of supporters. Identify and win over informal leaders or respected employees. Here, the network mapping done in Phase 1 comes in handy. Perhaps form a "shadow cabinet" of change ambassadors who are briefed on the plan early and can champion it among peers. Something I have used before in one of the companies I was leading was to ask HR to conduct a survey to

Phase 2: Planning

identify who would be interested in being a culture champion. We trained the selected individuals and evaluated their performance based on employee satisfaction, familiarity with goals and targets, and understanding of the strategic direction, including where the company is heading.

By Phase 2, some early skeptics might emerge ("We've seen initiatives fail before" or "The company is going to shut down"). Addressing their concerns openly and possibly incorporating feedback can turn detractors into neutral parties or even supporters. Ask them simple questions to hold them accountable, such as "What would you do to save it?" or "How can you participate in saving the company?" The CEO needs to be a role model, someone with the skill set to turn the company around, and this is not about degrees or experience. It is an ART, not a science. In planning, ensure that the forthcoming changes are supported by training plans (skill development) and a clear structure, such as the transformation office, so people know changes will be managed, not chaotic.

Additionally, manage *external stakeholder psychology*, including creditors, investors, and suppliers. Phase 2 often involves adversarial negotiations, such as requesting additional funding from investors like PIF or seeking restructuring from banks. Maintaining an optimistic yet realistic tone, backed by data, helps convince these parties to stay on board. If they sense the management team is in control and has a credible plan, they are more likely to extend trust. Conversely, if communication is poor, they may fear the worst and take aggressive actions (like calling loans due). Thus, a psychological aim in Phase 2 is to *project confidence and competence* to all stakeholders, internal and external. Internally, this might mean the CEO and leaders being visible and reinforcing, "We can and will turn this around together." Externally, it might involve carefully crafted messages about "strategic repositioning" rather than "desperation" to keep partners committed.

This also means you must approach the right people within these organizations who can back up your plan when the time comes. By understanding your network map, you can have a strategy to communicate with your stakeholders. To summarize, Phase 2 is not just a technical exercise of drawing plans on paper. It's about mentally preparing the organization to embrace the plan and ensuring everyone with a stake in the outcome feels engaged, respected, and cautiously hopeful as the company stands on the brink of significant change.

Final Deliverables for Phase 2: Planning

- The **Strategic Turnaround Framework** is a structured roadmap outlining financial, operational, and organizational transformation strategies to ensure alignment between vision and execution.
- **Scenario Planning and Risk Mitigation Strategy** is a contingency plan addressing best-case, base-case, and worst-case turnaround scenarios, ensuring agility in execution.
- The **Value Creation Playbook** is a prioritized set of initiatives designed to drive cost efficiency, revenue growth, and operational excellence.
- The **Financial Restructuring Plan** is a liquidity management, debt restructuring, and budget optimization strategy to stabilize cash flow and reduce financial risk.
- **Operations and Supply Chain Optimization** involves a plan to enhance efficiency, supplier renegotiations, and implement cost-saving initiatives to improve bottom-line results.
- A **Sales and Marketing Growth Strategy** is a roadmap for pricing, market positioning, and customer retention efforts to accelerate revenue generation.
- The **Leadership and Workforce Transformation Plan** serves as a blueprint for leadership restructuring, workforce realignment, and cultural revitalization to drive execution discipline.
- **Digital Transformation and IT Optimization** is a phased approach that involves automation, AI integration, and cybersecurity enhancements to improve business resilience.
- A **Stakeholder Engagement and Communication Plan** is a structured reporting and transparency framework that maintains trust among investors, lenders, and employees throughout the turnaround.
- The **Execution Governance and Accountability Model** is a milestone-driven tracking system to ensure disciplined execution, KPI monitoring, and leadership accountability.

Key Takeaways from Phase 2

1. **Strategy Must Translate into Actionable Plans:** A turnaround plan is only effective if it is practical, measurable, and executable. Each functional area (finance, operations, sales, IT) must have clear initiatives, timelines, and accountability frameworks to drive results.
2. **Prioritization Is Essential—Quick Wins Build Momentum:** The turnaround team must focus on early-stage wins that generate immediate cash flow improvements or cost savings. These quick wins demonstrate tangible progress to stakeholders and help fund long-term initiatives.
3. **Stakeholder Buy-In Determines Success:** A well-crafted plan is meaningless without stakeholder support. Ensuring that investors, creditors, employees, and customers understand and support the turnaround vision is critical for successful execution.
4. **Financial Restructuring Is as Important as Operational Efficiency:** Companies often focus solely on cutting costs but fail to address capital structure issues. Sustainable turnarounds require a balanced approach that improves cash flow while restructuring debt burdens.
5. **Execution Discipline Must Be Built Into the Plan:** Accountability structures, milestone tracking, and data-driven decision-making tools must be embedded into the turnaround plan to prevent execution failure. A Project Management Officer (PMO) or Chief Turnaround Officer ensures disciplined execution.
6. **Change Management and Communication Are Critical:** People resist change, especially in times of crisis. The most effective turnaround plans incorporate strong change management practices, transparent communication strategies, and cultural transformation initiatives to ensure buy-in at all organizational levels.
7. **Digital Transformation and AI Must Be Integrated:** Companies must leverage AI, automation, and digital tools to optimize costs, enhance customer engagement, and drive

efficiency. AI-powered predictive analytics, RPA-driven automation, and cloud-based IT solutions are no longer optional—they are key turnaround accelerators.
8. **The Plan Must Be Adaptive to External Market Forces:** Turnaround strategies should not be rigid—they must be adaptive to market disruptions, competitive shifts, and macroeconomic risks. Scenario planning ensures flexibility in decision-making while maintaining a clear focus on execution.
9. **Leadership Must Embody the Turnaround Vision:** Effective leadership drives a turnaround. The CEO, executive team, and department heads must demonstrate urgency, accountability, and resilience to inspire confidence internally and externally.
10. **Phase 2 Is the Foundation for Execution—No Room for Ambiguity:** By the end of Phase 2, every functional area should have a fully mapped-out strategy with designated owners, clear milestones, and well-defined KPIs. Ambiguity in planning leads to delays in execution. A well-structured Phase 2 ensures that Phase 3 (Implementation) runs efficiently.

Phase 3: Implementation

Phase 3 Overview: In Phase 3, the turnaround plan moves from paper to action. *Implementation* is where the organization executes the restructuring strategies explained in Phase 2. This phase is often the most challenging for many CEOs, and most fail (70 percent, according to an HBR study). The highest failure rates are in mature industries with significant structural challenges, companies with deeply entrenched organizational cultures, and businesses facing rapid technological disruption. It involves making tough changes, such as cutting costs (possibly resulting in job losses), launching new initiatives, renegotiating contracts, and addressing deep-seated cultural limitations—issues not identified in Phase 1 or planned for in Phase 2. It requires robust project management, relentless follow-up, and flexibility to troubleshoot problems on the fly—a skill you usually find in startup founders and teams. Phase 3 can span several months to a couple of years, depending on turnaround scope, but the first six to twelve months are typically critical to gain traction. I like to be aggressive, infuse the organization with shocking energy, and aim for a three- to nine-month period.

Key characteristics of this phase include establishing a Program Management Office (PMO) or a Transformation Office that directly reports to the CEO to track progress on all initiatives and provide regular reporting of results against the plan's milestones (often via weekly or monthly dashboards and, in critical cases, biweekly). Communication remains paramount: as changes roll out, the company must keep employees informed of what's happening and why and celebrate incremental successes to maintain morale.

Often, early in Phase 3, rapid results begin to show, such as the first successful cost reduction or an uptick in sales from a new marketing push. These should be highlighted (celebrated) as proof that the turnaround is working and building momentum. However, implementation can also face setbacks (a plan might not deliver as expected, or external conditions change), and the CEO needs to show positive momentum and reiterate the purpose and the charge to a forward path. Thus, Phase 3 requires agility—the plan may be tweaked in real time. For example, if a particular product's sales aren't recovering as hoped, management might decide to phase it out faster or increase its marketing efforts, depending on real-world feedback.

A notable example I recall is when we had a $50 billion stimulus package that was not moving according to the planned implementation, so we stopped all disbursements for two weeks while various initiatives continued. We changed the entire operating model and became more involved with the initiative owners every week, following the approach I would have taken in a portfolio company under similar circumstances. We brought all spending back on track and handled reporting to the board more transparently. It was a successful intervention that would not have happened if we had been rigid, not shown any flexibility, and not asked the initiative owners to be part of the solution. That kind of decisive execution exemplifies Phase 3. By the end of this phase, the company should see measurable improvements in its financials and operations, confirming that the steps taken are yielding a healthier enterprise poised for the final phase of sustained growth.

Executing Restructuring Plans

This sub-section covers the nuts and bolts of carrying out the restructuring:

Phase 3: Implementation

a. Project Management and Governance: Right at the start of Phase 3, set up a *Turnaround PMO or Transformative Officer under the CEO* if not already in place. This office/officer tracks all initiatives defined in Phase 2, monitors KPIs, and keeps everyone accountable. The plan's initiatives should now be broken into actionable tasks with owners and deadlines. Use tools like Gantt charts or project management software to visualize the timetable. Hold weekly or biweekly *SteerCo* (Steering Committee) *meetings* with top leadership and initiative owners to review progress, resolve bottlenecks, and make decisions quickly. The governance should also be robust enough, especially if there is a cash squeeze or ongoing assessment, while operations must continue. Hence, I would further set an Operational Risk and Procurement Committee (mandated to remain conscious of the operation while ensuring recommended procurement orders are being scrutinized before they go up to the CEO or SteerCo, which is preferable for me), HR, Hiring, and Culture Committee to deal with cultural challenges, as well as hiring and layoffs. Four to five committees should bring transparency and accountability across the organization.

This should also be evaluated to prevent delays in vital decisions, and maybe have a defined key decision path, items for the critical path, and responsible people for the path. This governance structure ensures that issues encountered in one area (e.g., procurement can't renegotiate a contract as much as hoped) are escalated and alternative actions are decided upon, such as finding a different supplier. Essentially, the turnaround should be treated like a program with multiple interdependent projects. Rigorous management is needed to keep it on track. Consulting firms often help clients by running these PMOs and bringing in experienced project leaders to coordinate. This is now the best practice in the KSA government.

b. Financial Restructuring Execution: If the plan involves financial moves, such as debt refinancing, asset sales, or cost cuts, those are executed here. For debt, this means *negotiating with creditors* to finalize new terms or going through legal processes, such as a formal bankruptcy or insolvency proceeding. It might involve issuing new equity or converting debt to equity as agreed upon. For asset sales, hire investment bankers or run sale processes to sell divisions or real estate as identified. Execution means closing those deals and getting the cash in. Implementing cost cuts involves carrying out layoffs, shutting down facilities, and terminating leases according to legal protocols and timelines. These actions must be carefully managed to avoid business disruption and should be brought to a final decision at the SteerCo level for final debate. For instance, if closing a plant, ensure production is smoothly ramped down and shifted elsewhere, and communicate with customers to reassure them of supply continuity. Document the savings achieved and update budgets accordingly. Each financial action completed is a milestone (e.g., "sold X units for $Y million by Q3; used proceeds to pay down debt, reducing interest expense by X percent"). It's crucial to continuously forecast the cash impact of these moves against the plan to ensure the company remains solvent throughout implementation.

During its 2005–2007 bankruptcy, Delta Air Lines, for example, shed billions of dollars in costs by renegotiating aircraft leases and cutting jobs. The execution was phased to ensure that service levels were maintained. The lesson is to implement financial restructurings in a controlled manner with stakeholder communication at every step. Therefore, employees, suppliers, and investors aren't caught off guard by a facility closure announcement. Any risk of this has been addressed in the premortem documents of Phase 2, and necessary actions or decisions are made at the SteerCo level if needed, although not to bottleneck decisions.

c. Operational Changes Rollout: Implementing operational improvements means adopting new processes and systems. If Lean projects are planned, Phase 3 would be when Kaizen events happen on the floor, new Standard Operating Procedures (SOPs) are issued, and equipment upgrades or maintenance catch-up are performed. It might involve temporarily slowing production to reconfigure a line or train workers on new methods. For each operational initiative, have a clear checklist, such as implementing the Total Productive Maintenance (TPM) program in Plant A. Step 1: Form maintenance teams. Step 2: Schedule a preventative maintenance calendar. Step 3: Train teams. Step 4: Measure downtime improvements monthly.

Phase 3: Implementation

Track results closely. If the scrap rate goes down or output per hour goes up, document it and ensure it sustained. Maybe roll out a new IT system or customer service protocol for service processes, accompanied by training and a pilot period to work out the kinks. A critical part is monitoring KPIs, such as daily throughput, defect rates, and customer wait times, to gauge if changes yield expected benefits. If not, adjust quickly—it's common to iterate during Phase 3. One helpful approach is running *pilots* for big changes, such as testing a new inventory system in one warehouse before a full rollout. That pilot feedback can improve the implementation plan for broader deployment. By the end of Phase 3, all significant operational changes (plant closures, new systems, process improvements) should be completed or well underway, with performance metrics trending positively (e.g., unit costs down 10 percent, delivery times cut in half).

One of the methods I like to follow to assess operations and maximize performance is the *Theory of Constraints.* (Note: The methodology applies across various industries, from manufacturing to service sectors, with consistent core principles.) Below is a process I developed and followed, for example, with a local Saudi AC manufacturer:

Operational Assessment Using the Theory of Constraints

Step-by-Step Operational Assessment Process

a. **Identify the System's Constraint**
   - Where is the weakest link in the operational chain?
   - What is preventing the system from achieving its goal?
   - Check for:
     - Physical constraints (equipment, capacity)
     - Policy constraints (rules, procedures)
     - Market constraints (demand, sales)
     - Management constraints (decision-making processes)

b. **Exploit the Constraint**
   - Maximize existing constraints' efficiency with minimal investment
   - Strategies include:

- Reducing idle time
  - Eliminating non-value-added activities
  - Ensuring the constraint is always working at optimal capacity
  - Minimizing interruptions and downtimes

c. **Subordinate Everything Else to the Constraint**
   - Align the entire system to support the constraint's performance.
   - Adjust other processes to:
     - Ensure a smooth flow to the constraint.
     - Prevent overproduction.
     - Match the pace of the constraint.
     - Create a balanced system that doesn't overwhelm or starve the constraint.

d. **Elevate the Constraint**
   - Make significant investments to increase the constraint's capacity.
   - Consider:
     - adding resources
     - upgrading equipment
     - implementing new technologies
     - hiring additional skilled personnel
     - expanding capabilities
     - Hire a strong CFO

e. **Prevent Constraint Inactivity**
   - Once the current constraint is resolved, prevent complacency.
   - Continuous improvement steps:
     - Recognize that the constraint will shift.
     - Regularly reassess the system.
     - Be prepared to repeat the process with the new constraint.
     - Maintain a culture of ongoing improvement.

Phase 3: Implementation

f. **Key Metrics to Monitor**
   - Throughput: how quickly your business makes money from sales
   - Inventory: money you spend buying products that you plan to sell later
   - Operational Expense: money you spend to convert your inventory into sales (like worker salaries, electricity, equipment costs)

g. **Practical Implementation Guidelines**
   - Focus on system-wide optimization, not local efficiencies.
   - Challenge existing assumptions and traditional cost accounting methods.
   - Communicate changes clearly across the organization.
   - Develop a holistic view of operations.

h. **Common Pitfalls to Avoid**
   - optimizing non-constrained resources
   - ignoring the interdependencies between processes
   - failing to create a supportive organizational culture
   - treating constraints as permanent or unchangeable

i. **Philosophical Approach**
   - Constraints are not negative but opportunities for improvement. The goal is to:
     - Understand the system's performance.
     - Systematically improve its capability.
     - Create a culture of continuous learning and adaptation.

Financial Restructuring Execution

a. **Liquidity and Working Capital Optimization**
   i. **Daily Cash Flow Tracking:**
      a. **Implement Real-Time Cash Dashboards**
         a. **Develop an *automated real-time liquidity dashboard***

that consolidates bank balances, upcoming receivables, and financial obligations in a single view.
  b. Use *AI-driven cash flow forecasting models* to predict short-term liquidity gaps based on historical trends and seasonal fluctuations.
  c. Ensure daily *bank reconciliations* to prevent discrepancies and missing transactions.
b. **Prioritize Cash Preservation Strategies (e.g., renegotiating supplier payments, invoice factoring)**
  a. **Extend supplier payment terms** by negotiating deferred payments for critical vendors while offering early-payment discounts to strategic suppliers.
  b. **Evaluate invoice factoring** where necessary. Sell outstanding invoices to third-party financiers for immediate liquidity while balancing financing costs.
  c. **Freeze nonessential spending**, such as marketing or discretionary IT upgrades, until cash flow stabilizes.
c. **Accounts Payable and Accounts Receivable Management**
  a. **Implement a structured approval workflow** for AP/AR processes to prevent unnecessary spending and ensure timely collections.
  b. **Categorize outstanding payments** based on priority: critical expenses (payroll, rent, debt servicing), operational costs, and discretionary spending.
  c. **Track aged receivables daily**, setting strict internal deadlines for outstanding invoices.
d. **Enforce Stricter Payment Collection from Clients**
  a. **Introduce a tiered escalation system**—friendly reminders at seven, fourteen, and thirty days overdue, followed by legal notices for longer defaults.
  b. **Offer early payment discounts** to high-value clients while enforcing penalties on overdue payments.
  c. **Assign dedicated AR personnel or AI-powered collection tools** to automate payment follow-ups and reduce outstanding debts.

Phase 3: Implementation

   e. **Reduce Outstanding Receivables** by negotiating early payment incentives.
      a. **Provide structured discounted payment plans** for large clients who commit to early settlements (e.g., 2 percent discount for payments within ten days).
      b. **Convert overdue receivables into structured installment payment plans** to improve partial cash recovery rather than full defaults.
      c. **Implement "cash-on-delivery" or advance payment policies** for at-risk customers to mitigate further outstanding receivables.

b. **Debt Restructuring Execution**
   i. **Secure Loan Extensions or Covenant Waivers Where Needed**
      a. **Prepare a detailed cash flow and business viability report** before approaching lenders, demonstrating debt repayment feasibility over an extended period.
      b. **Request a temporary covenant waiver** to avoid technical default on financial obligations, justifying it with operational restructuring progress.
      c. **Convert short-term loans into long-term facilities** to reduce the monthly cash flow burden.
   ii. **Evaluate Debt Refinancing Options Through PE-Backed Capital Injections or Asset-Based Lending**
      a. **Assess Private Equity (PE) funding interest**, focusing on turnaround funds or *distressed asset investors* willing to inject fresh equity in exchange for ownership restructuring.
      b. **Explore asset-backed financing**, leveraging real estate, machinery, or high-value inventory to *secure working capital loans* without increasing unsecured liabilities.
      c. **Evaluate bridge loans** from short-term lenders to cover operational needs while executing a longer-term debt restructuring plan.

c. **Capital Raising** (if needed):
   i. **Finalize Equity Raises, Private Debt Placements, or Asset Sales to Secure Liquidity**
      a. **Identify potential equity investors**, such as venture capital, PE firms, or strategic investors, and tailor the turnaround pitch to their risk appetite.
      b. **Structure convertible debt instruments** that offer investors downside protection while securing immediate liquidity without significant ownership dilution.
      c. **Conduct a portfolio review** to identify *non-core assets* (real estate, patents, underperforming subsidiaries) for strategic liquidation to raise emergency cash.

d. **Vendor and Supplier Payment Strategy:**
   i. **Implement Staggered Payment Plans to Manage Short-Term Cash Constraints**
      a. **Categorize suppliers** into *critical*, *strategic*, and *discretionary* groups, prioritizing essential vendors for timely payments while extending terms for others.
      b. **Offer structured repayment agreements** with staggered installments (e.g., 30/60/90-day payments) to prevent *supplier contract termination*.
      c. **Leverage supply chain financing**, where financial institutions pay suppliers upfront, and the company repays them later with extended terms.

Deliverables:

- **Weekly Liquidity Dashboards & Variance Reports:** real-time financial tracking systems highlighting current liquidity, cash flow projections, and unexpected variances to enable proactive decision-making.
- **Negotiation Tracker for Debt Restructuring and Capital-Raising Efforts:** a structured, documented tracker capturing lender discussions, debt restructuring status, investor

Phase 3: Implementation

negotiations, and capital-raising progress to ensure accountability and transparency.

Monitoring and Performance Tracking

As changes are implemented, *continuous monitoring* is essential to ensure the turnaround stays on course:

- **Key Performance Indicators (KPIs) Dashboards:** Set up real-time or weekly dashboards to track the metrics defined in the plan. These might include financial KPIs (cash balance, EBITDA, revenue run rate), operational KPIs (production volume, backlog, quality metrics), and market KPIs (order intake, customer satisfaction scores). By comparing these to targets and prior periods, management can quickly see where things are improving or lagging. For instance, if daily sales are not increasing as expected after a marketing campaign, that's a flag to investigate and tweak the strategy. The dashboard should be cascaded, e.g., to a high level for execs and more granular for line managers.

  Many companies use simple tools like Excel or more sophisticated BI software to aggregate data from various departments. The PMO usually compiles this. Publish the results internally, such as a weekly email update, "Turnaround Tracker," that shows progress. This transparency keeps urgency high and encourages problem-solving (no one wants their metric in red week after week). It's akin to a scorecard for the whole team—everyone can rally around improving it. Here are a few things I usually implement: cross-C-level KPIs responsibilities to enhance and reinforce interdependencies between executives, develop leading indicators where data availability allows it, and monitor and prevent problems from happening before they happen.

- **Regular Review Cadence:** Establish a cadence of performance reviews. At a minimum, the executive team should deliver a *monthly review* of the overall turnaround status along with more frequent reviews (even daily or weekly) for critical metrics such as cash flow. These meetings will focus on variances: where actual results differ from the plan and why. If cost savings are behind schedule, is it because an initiative is delayed? If so, determine where leading indicators can be developed to track performance and identify potential issues early.

For example, we once launched a funding initiative for a bank that financed mortgages as part of a government program. To establish a baseline, we analyzed previous data on key metrics such as:

- the average number of people visiting the mortgage bank
- the time required to process applications
- approval rates
- disbursement timelines

To monitor real-time performance, we implemented a technology-driven solution: an iPad system that tracked daily activity and alerted us to deviations from expected trends. Whenever an issue arose—such as a drop in approval rates or delays in processing—we immediately contacted the mortgage bank to address the problem. This proactive approach helped us keep performance on track and meet our target sales.

Consider using a "flash report" approach—quick, frequent reporting of a few vital signs— when it is challenging to develop leading indicators (e.g., cash, sales, production), combined with more in-depth monthly reports. For governance, consider establishing sub-committees (finance, operational risk, and procurement) that meet biweekly to dive into their respective areas, then report to a main monthly steering committee. This layered approach ensures issues are addressed at the right level. Keep minutes and action items. This creates accountability by assigning action item owners and deadlines for each issue to be resolved or an initiative to recover, bringing the plan back on track. Here is the mantra: *no news is **not** good news*. The PMO should surface even minor concerns early to fix them before they become big problems.

• **Risk Management During Implementation:** Even with a great plan, risks and unexpected challenges are likely to arise in Phase 3. The monitoring process should include a risk tracker and a ready resolution plan when the risk occurs. Identify key risks, e.g., "If our product relaunch in Q4 fails to boost sales, we will miss revenue targets," or "Government intervention, layoffs, and lawsuits could slow cost reduction." Assign owners to each risk to develop contingency plans. For the product relaunch example, a contingency might include a backup marketing campaign or a strategy to promote an alternative product. For labor issues, a contingency might be engaging a third-party government mediator or preparing financial buffers in case negotiations protract.

Regularly update the status of each risk in review meetings. Essentially, hope for the best outcomes but prepare for the worst. By performing the premortem and thinking ahead, the team won't be caught flat-footed. Also, stay alert to external factors: if the economy shifts or a pandemic introduces new risks, be ready to adapt the plan. One practical tip is to maintain a modest cash reserve or access to emergency funding during Phase 3 as a buffer for unforeseen expenses. This financial risk mitigation can be a lifesaver if a critical machine fails or a new competitor's move forces an unplanned response. Successful turnaround implementations are dynamic; they require a tight grip on performance and a willingness to pivot as needed without losing sight of the end goals.

Deliverables:

- **Sales Incentive Plan Implementation**: a structured rollout of revised sales incentives designed to drive *immediate revenue impact*. This ensures that sales teams are aligned with turnaround goals, motivated by performance-based rewards, and focused on high-priority customer segments.
- **Revenue Impact Report from New Customer Acquisition and Retention Strategies**: a detailed report measuring the effectiveness of customer acquisition efforts and retention strategies. This report tracks conversion rates, customer lifetime value, and churn reduction, ensuring that the turnaround delivers sustainable revenue growth rather than short-term spikes.
- **Risk Report (Actual and Possible) with Actionable Solutions**: a live risk management document that identifies emerging challenges, assesses their potential impact, and outlines contingency plans. Each risk has an assigned owner, a mitigation plan, and a resolution timeline, ensuring issues are addressed before they escalate into critical failures.

- **Monitoring Dashboard with KPIs, Leading Indicators, and Other Related Reports**: a centralized, real-time dashboard tracking financial, operational, and market KPIs, along with leading indicators that predict future performance. This ensures that management has instant visibility of the business's health, enabling quick interventions to keep the turnaround on track and adaptive to changing conditions.

Leadership and Workforce Engagement

Implementing a turnaround is as much about *people leading change* as it is about executing tasks:

- **Visible Leadership and Communication:** During Phase 3, the CEO and C-level leaders must be highly visible on the front lines. This means plant visits, town hall meetings, and regular communications about progress and next steps. Employees are going through possibly the most tumultuous time in their careers; seeing leaders present, listening, and acknowledging the hard work goes a long way. For example, if layoffs occurred, leaders should spend time with the remaining teams (survivors) to address "survivor's guilt" and refocus them on the mission ahead. Consistent messaging is key: reiterate the vision of the turnaround, why the sacrifices are necessary, and paint a picture of what success looks like. For example, "If we stay on track, by next year we will be back to profitability and able to invest in growth, securing everyone's future." Sometimes, pausing to realign and energize the workforce yields better execution afterward if needed.

- **Employee Empowerment in Execution:** Encourage a culture where employees at all levels can suggest improvements and take the initiative. I usually have three channels to communicate with the organization: a Direct Channel for all direct reports, such as n-2 and n-3, where they can connect one-to-one, once a month organization-level townhall where employees are encouraged and rewarded for participation and throwing around ideas, and an anonymous channel for those who are shy or have concerns they do not want to be made public. Three channels are additions to HR and culture channels.

Often, frontline workers are aware of quick fixes or innovations that management might overlook. For example, in one of my previous roles, I reviewed a business plan for a company asset with the executive team. The plan showed low returns, and the CIO insisted that this asset would not generate higher returns. So, I created a three-stage plan, inviting cross-department individuals from various levels of the organization. In the first stage, we all met, and each individual had to present three ideas related to our problem, and no one was allowed to judge the ideas. In Stage 2, we reviewed each idea individually and evaluated it. In Stage 3, we selected and implemented the top solution(s) for our problem. This exercise resulted in the asset generating more money than expected and taught everyone a lesson about collaborating and speaking up. Setting up channels for ideas (like an internal "ideas portal" or regular team huddles where suggestions are solicited) can unleash solutions that help the turnaround.

Moreover, giving teams autonomy to achieve their targets can improve outcomes. For instance, a call center team might find a better way to handle customer complaints that reduces churn. Recognizing and rewarding these contributions publicly fuels a positive cycle of engagement. One technique is creating cross-functional "tiger teams" or problem-solving squads for specific challenges, which empowers employees to own parts of the turnaround. For example, if on-time delivery is an issue, form a team from operations, logistics, and sales to diagnose and fix it. By entrusting them, you get better insight and deepen their commitment to overall success.

- **Training and Support:** As new processes or systems roll out, ensure that employees are not left behind. Implementation often fails if people aren't confident in doing things the new way. So, invest in training sessions, on-the-job coaching, and precise documentation. If a new IT system is introduced to manage inventory or CRM, schedule multiple training waves, and have a help desk or "floor walkers" to assist when it goes live. For any relocated or restructured teams, consider team-building or reorientation programs. Also, provide emotional support where needed —turning around a company can be stressful and lead to burnout. HR should be part of the implementation governance, monitoring morale, and helping address concerns, such as adjusting workloads if someone is overwhelmed or providing counseling services if stress is high.

When I tasked one of my organizations with the high-pressure challenge of simultaneously scaling up and executing more than eleven transactions, I ensured that HR and the Culture Committee were part of my plan, bringing a dedicated specialist, a specialized therapist, and a career coach to provide support. I also dedicated several C-level members to provide mentoring and guidance, and brought in consultants to support the extra workload. This helped the organization cope with the temporary pressure. In short, treat employees as essential partners in execution: give them the necessary tools, skills, and motivation to carry out the plan, and they will often exceed expectations.

Deliverables:

i. **Leadership Performance Review Metrics**
   a. Have a structured evaluation system to assess leadership visibility, communication effectiveness, and execution discipline during the turnaround.
   b. KPIs include leadership presence on the ground (e.g., number of town halls, direct employee engagements), transparency in communication, and decision-making agility.
   c. This metric ensures executives are actively driving cultural alignment, workforce motivation, and operational resilience throughout Phase 3.

ii. **Employee Engagement Survey Results and Action Plan**
   a. Conduct a quantitative and qualitative assessment capturing workforce morale, participation in turnaround initiatives, and the effectiveness of internal communication.
   b. The action plan should directly outline improvements based on employee feedback, for example, between the n-2 level and the CEO, ensuring that concerns are addressed in real-time while reinforcing alignment with turnaround goals.
   c. Tracking improvements in cross-functional collaboration, training effectiveness, and workforce empowerment initiatives ensures engagement drives execution success.

Phase 3: Implementation

Risk Management and Contingency Planning

In any planning I undertake, I remain mindful of both my own and others' blind spots—after all, investment is the art of maximizing returns relative to risk. To address this, as I mentioned earlier, I would have each department head list the possible risks and issues we would face—not only operational but also organizational, staffing, political, and other relevant factors. We would then meet with SteerCo to ensure that we have outlined all possible reasons for failure and developed a potential remedy for each. I call it "tell me all the ways we can die before we do"—a premortem analysis in less dramatic names (some dramatic words are also essential to create a sense of urgency). This simple and effective exercise helps the employees and the company be ready to handle crises or setbacks so they don't derail the turnaround:

- **Active Risk Monitoring:** As mentioned in monitoring, keep a live risk register. This subsection reiterates the importance of the risk and details some likely risks. For instance, identify legal risks (ongoing lawsuits could impact finances), operational risks (a major equipment failure or supply chain disruption), market risks (a new competitor or loss of a big customer), and even political and regulatory risks (new laws that could affect the business). Assign a "risk owner" for each category, often a senior executive, who periodically reports on that risk. Use leading indicators to foresee issues. Monitor quality metrics to identify if product issues are increasing, which could signal a potential recall risk, or maintain close contact with the top tier customers to sense if they are unhappy or intend to leave. For example, a manufacturing turnaround should closely monitor safety metrics; a serious accident could halt operations and incur significant costs. If near-misses increase, intervene immediately (perhaps with emergency safety training) to prevent bigger problems.

- **Contingency Plans:** Have a Plan B (and Plan C) ready for each high-priority risk. If a critical initiative fails to deliver, what then? For example, if the plan assumes a successful asset sale by Q2 and it falls through, the contingency might be an alternate buyer pipeline or a temporary bridge loan arrangement. If a new product launch is delayed, consider a marketing push of existing products as a fallback to meet revenue goals.

Contingency planning could also mean preparing for worst-case scenarios. For example, if the turnaround doesn't restore liquidity fast enough, be ready to approach the **Bankruptcy Committee** in the government in a controlled manner rather than a chaotic collapse. While that's undesirable, having a prepackaged bankruptcy plan in your back pocket can be prudent if the situation is touch-and-go. The playbook should outline who will decide when to trigger contingencies and how communication will be handled. (Stakeholders should know that "if X happens, we will do Y" to reduce panic.) Nothing should catch the team completely off guard. Even if something unexpected occurs, the mindset of proactive problem-solving and scenario planning established in Phase 3 will enable a nimble response.

• **External Expert Support:** Recognize when you might need external help during implementation—particularly when the team lacks expertise, the right skill sets, or is facing possible key departures. Sometimes, companies hire consultants or interim specialists to address specific challenges (e.g., an IT expert to implement a system quickly or a legal advisor to handle complex negotiations). The plan should earmark areas where outside support could be critical and establish those relationships in advance. It's part of contingency to know your limits. If a PR crisis erupts, such as negative media coverage about the turnaround, having a PR agency on standby to assist is wise. Ideally, this would be the same agency that developed a communication strategy in the Planning Phase. Similarly, if restructuring the supply chain, consider partnering with a logistics firm to temporarily manage distribution. This can help mitigate internal chaos that may arise during the reorganization process. By Phase 3, some of these external supports might already be engaged, such as a turnaround consultant guiding the whole process. However, ensure flexibility to increase support if needed when risks materialize.

Program Governance and Turnaround:

Establishing a Turnaround Office (TO)

Global best practices form a central Turnaround Office to coordinate all workstreams (financial, operational, sales, HR, digital) and ensure accountability:

Phase 3: Implementation

- Members: Includes the CRO or interim executive lead, CFO, a representative from each key function, plus a project manager from the CEO's office, if applicable
- Weekly Steering Committee Meetings: Reviews a "milestone RAG dashboard" (Red-Amber-Green) for each initiative, tracks issues, and highlights needed decisions
- PMO Tools: Maintain a consolidated timeline, risk register, and escalation matrix

This ensures rigorous execution discipline, prompt issue resolution, and consistent communication across departments.

Deliverables:

- **Crisis Response Action Plan**: a structured preemptive crisis management framework outlining high-risk scenarios, mitigation strategies, and escalation procedures. This plan ensures that risks are actively monitored, allowing the company to respond swiftly to operational disruptions, financial instability, or reputational crises.
- **Legal Compliance Audit Report**: a comprehensive legal and regulatory assessment identifying potential compliance gaps, legal risks, and action plans for mitigation. The report includes an analysis of ongoing litigation risks, contract review processes, and industry-specific compliance standards, ensuring proactive legal risk management throughout the turnaround.
- **Turnaround Office (TO) Governance Framework:** a structured operational playbook for the Turnaround Office detailing the scope, responsibilities, and reporting cadence of the turnaround leadership team. This framework ensures that financial, operational, and strategic workstreams are aligned, driving execution discipline.
- **Risk Register and Escalation Matrix:** a live document tracking all identified risks, their potential impact, and pre-approved escalation paths. This ensures that senior leadership can intervene promptly when risks materialize, preventing minor issues from snowballing into major disruptions.

Psychological Dynamics in Phase 3 (Implementation)

Phase 3 is the make-or-break period emotionally for an organization. Employees will experience layoffs, restructurings, and new ways of working, which can be turbulent. Managing the collective psyche is about maintaining morale, building resilience, and overcoming resistance.

One key psychological challenge is the phenomenon of *change fatigue*. Midway through implementation, people might feel exhausted or overwhelmed by continuous changes. To combat this, leadership should gauge team sentiment regularly (through surveys or manager check-ins) and adjust the pace as necessary. Sometimes, staggering initiatives a bit can help teams catch their breath. Celebrating small wins becomes vital now: each time a milestone is hit (e.g., a successful product launch or a cost target met), hold a brief celebration or at least a congratulatory communication. This injects positive energy and reminds everyone that progress is happening. It reinforces the line of sight between their hard work and company improvement, which is motivating.

Another aspect is dealing with *resistance or setbacks* without losing momentum. Not everyone will embrace every change; some may quietly revert to old habits or voice negativity ("This new process doesn't work," etc.). The change ambassadors or coalition of supporters cultivated in Phase 2 should be activated to address this. Peer influence can be effective. For example, if a veteran employee is skeptical, pairing them with a younger, enthusiastic team member on a project can sometimes shift attitudes through peer learning. Additionally, maintain an open-door policy that encourages employees to voice concerns or ideas for improvement. When people feel heard, they are more likely to support the decisions even if they disagree because they at least have input.

Transparency is still crucial—share both good and bad news. If something isn't going well (perhaps a plan target has been missed), management should acknowledge it and explain the corrective action rather than hide it. This honesty prevents the grapevine from spinning worse stories and shows competence ("Yes, we're behind on X, but here's what we're doing about it"). It also invites employees to contribute solutions—turning potential

Phase 3: Implementation

cynics into problem solvers. A cultural win in Phase 3 occurs when employees start thinking and acting like "owners" of the turnaround, not just pawns. You may see this when *front-line teams* create mini turnaround plans for their department, or when employees voluntarily work extra hours to ensure a critical task is done. These are signs that the organization has bought into the change psychologically. Most importantly, do not delay letting go of a person who is not moving forward after giving them a chance to do so.

Leaders should also be mindful of the impact of stress and burnout on their teams. Encourage work-life balance even amid the push for initiatives like mandating a no-meeting hour or an occasional long weekend after a big deadline. Small gestures of appreciation (like the CEO personally thanking a team that pulled off a big project) can alleviate stress by making people feel valued. In troubled times, emotions run high; there may be moments of conflict or doubt. Leaders must remain calm, empathetic, and steadfast, demonstrating emotional intelligence and resilience. They must show empathy for those who lost colleagues in layoffs or those struggling to adapt, while rallying everyone around the hopeful narrative of the turnaround succeeding. It's a delicate balance of being human and being resolute.

In summary, the psychological dimension of Phase 3 involves converting the initial urgency and plans into a sustained can-do culture and cleansing any doubters by either changing them or letting them go. The organization should emerge from implementation, not only having executed the tasks but also with a stronger, more cohesive culture that believes in itself. If Phase 3 is handled well on the people side, by Phase 4, the workforce will be re-energized, proud of what they accomplished, and ready to carry the improvements forward.

Final Deliverables of Phase 3

i. **Execution Progress Dashboard**
    a. A *real-time tracking system* monitors the status of restructuring initiatives, cost-saving measures, and revenue growth efforts.
    b. This ensures transparent visibility for leadership and

stakeholders, enabling quick interventions when or before deviations occur from the turnaround plan.
  ii. **Financial and Operational Reports**
     a. Periodic updates on liquidity, cost reduction achievements, revenue performance, and operational KPIs to measure financial recovery.
     b. These reports provide actionable insights that inform strategic adjustments and resource allocation, enabling sustained momentum.
  iii. **Stakeholder Confidence Score**
     a. A structured assessment capturing employee morale, investor sentiment, and customer trust in the turnaround process.
     b. This metric ensures that leadership can address concerns proactively and reinforce stakeholder alignment with the company's recovery trajectory.

Key Takeaways from Phase 3

- **Execution Defines Success:** Even the best turnaround plans fail if execution is weak. Phase 3 requires leadership, discipline, urgency, and adaptability to drive meaningful change.
- **Data-Driven Decisions Are Critical:** Companies must track KPIs in real time, adjust quickly based on insights, and use leading indicators to prevent crises before they occur.
- **Accountability and Leadership Drive Results:** A robust governance framework, clear ownership of initiatives, and decisive leadership ensure that execution stays on course.
- **Stakeholder Trust Is an Asset:** Transparent communication with employees, investors, and customers builds confidence and buy-in, reducing resistance to change and reinforcing long-term commitment to success.

Phase 4: Sustainability and Growth

In Phase 3 (Implementation), we execute financial restructuring, operational optimizations, leadership changes, and stakeholder engagement strategies. However, a successful turnaround must transition into a sustain-

Phase 3: Implementation

able growth model to ensure long-term stability, profitability, and resilience against future risks.

Phase 4 (Sustainability and Growth) focuses on embedding improvements into the company's DNA, ensuring continuous performance monitoring, and creating a culture of agility and innovation. This phase is where the company needs to grow beyond its current leadership and ensure that its DNA changes are in place for the long-term survival of the company.

Phase 4: Sustainability and Growth

Phase 4 Overview: Phase 4 focuses on solidifying the gains from the turnaround and transitioning the company back onto a path of *sustainable growth*. The crisis should be passed; the company should be financially stable and more efficient. The focus shifts to *long-term strategies*, including scaling innovation, expanding into new markets, creating a sustainable governance model, and continually improving operations so that the company not only avoids slipping back into trouble but actively thrives. It pivots from reactive fixes to proactive growth initiatives, turning the turnaround into a lasting competitive advantage.

A central theme in Phase 4 is embedding a culture of continuous improvement and agility. The structures and processes introduced during the turnaround (like KPI tracking, cross-functional teamwork, accountability, and rigorous financial discipline) should be institutionalized to become "the way we do business." The organization also reflects and learns from the turnaround journey. Perhaps updating its mission or values to emphasize resilience, accountability, and customer focus was key to the recovery. Phase 4 often involves strategic growth moves: once the core is healthy, the company may pursue new product development, acquisitions, or expansion that were previously put on hold. It's critical, however, to apply

Phase 4: Sustainability and Growth 89

the rigorous analysis from earlier phases to these decisions, ensuring the company doesn't overextend recklessly.

Think of Phase 4 as graduating from triage to fitness training: the company can now focus on strengthening and building muscle (you can tell by now I love working out). The outcome of Phase 4 is a business that not only has recovered but is positioned for long-term success, with stakeholders confident in its governance and direction. The success is communicated publicly to financial institutions and others, bringing proud moments to employees, their families, and the wider community. In places like Saudi Arabia, this holds significant value as it provides easier funding terms for Phase 4 and ensures the company's recent history is not forgotten. It's the final validation of the turnaround: when the company achieves consistent profitable growth and perhaps even exceeds industry benchmarks, proving that the transformation is sustainable.

1. Financial Sustainability and Capital Structure Optimization

Strengthening Liquidity and Working Capital Management Building: Long-term liquidity resilience is essential to sustaining gains from the turnaround and preparing for future disruptions. Embedding real-time cash tracking tools into daily financial reporting systems allows management to monitor liquidity in granular detail. This extends beyond high-level cash balances and includes dynamic visibility into inflows, outflows, payment timings, and operational bottlenecks affecting working capital.

A rolling thirteen-week cash forecast is a globally accepted framework that links strategic and operational decisions to short-term liquidity. It offers early visibility into potential cash gaps, enabling preemptive action. Forecasts should be refreshed weekly and linked to KPIs across procurement, AR/AP cycles, and sales conversion.

Establishing emergency credit lines or access to standby facilities is crucial for effective financial management. These credit arrangements must be negotiated when the company's performance improves and lenders are more open, with long-term rates that are more favorable. The rates in 2025 are still acceptable but high compared to those of the last decade. The goal is to reduce dependency on reactive, high-cost funding options during future downturns.

Other critical practices include setting cash collection targets per department (especially in B2B), tightening billing cycles, and incentivizing customers to pay early via discounts or digital payment options. Monitoring working capital efficiency using metrics, such as Cash Conversion Cycle (CCC), Days Sales Outstanding (DSO), and Inventory Turnover, becomes an institutional practice at this stage.

This framework ensures the company doesn't fall into short-termism or liquidity stress—two common pitfalls that reverse successful turnarounds.

Long-Term Debt Management

A sustainable company must reduce leverage while optimizing its capital structure to support growth. After stabilizing, the firm should focus on smart refinancing — extending maturity profiles and lowering average interest costs.

Following the turnaround, creditworthiness typically improves, giving access to better lending terms. Management should proactively engage with credit rating agencies and financial institutions to refinance legacy debt, swap short-term instruments for long-term fixed-rate debt, or convert variable-rate exposure into fixed-rate debt, depending on where interest rates are projected to be. I am also a strong advocate for diversifying funding sources and tapping into multiple sources, such as Sukuk or private credit, while maintaining strong strategic relationships with those institutions that have shown flexibility and support during the turnaround phase.

Setting a target debt-to-equity ratio as part of the capital allocation strategy document developed earlier acts as a guardrail. This ratio should align with industry norms and investor expectations while factoring in macroeconomic risks. Simultaneously, the firm should benchmark itself against the best-in-class capital structures of its peers.

A structured engagement model with lenders and Zukuk/bondholders is vital. Regular updates, clear financial communication, and preemptive

Phase 4: Sustainability and Growth

covenant monitoring build trust. In the event of future distress, this credibility becomes a powerful lever.

Additionally, firms should monitor capital intensity to evaluate when and how to raise capital. For example, industrial companies with heavy capital expenditure (capex) needs must synchronize their funding and operating cycles. Technology firms may benefit more from growth equity or hybrid mezzanine structures that delay dilution, allowing them to retain ownership and control. With advancements in technology and regulations in Saudi Arabia, real estate can utilize blockchain technology to start converting receivables and provide fractional sale and lease contracts.

Ultimately, debt is not inherently bad—but poorly managed debt is. An optimized debt profile builds resilience without constraining strategic flexibility, and hiring or having the right CFO is crucial in this regard. This is a skill we lack in the kingdom, as most companies view this function as more closely related to accounting than strategy.

Profitability and Cost Discipline Framework

i. Once initial turnaround savings are captured, Phase 4 focuses on institutionalizing cost discipline without stifling growth. Zero-Based Budgeting (ZBB) becomes a key enabler. Unlike incremental budgeting, ZBB requires every expense to be justified from scratch each year. This drives sharper alignment between resource allocation and business priorities, linking them to the overall C-level targeted KPIs. Therefore, they are all responsible for it.

ii. To be effective, ZBB must be digitally enabled (e.g., tools that simulate the ROI of proposed budgets) and culturally embraced. Managers should be trained to prioritize value over volume. Central cost control offices (e.g., transformation PMOs at the CEO's office) can help standardize templates and improve forecasting accuracy.

In parallel, the continuous pursuit of gross margin improvement is essential. This may involve pricing optimization through AI and redesigning products to reduce the cost of goods sold. Unit economics must be analyzed frequently, especially in fast-evolving sectors, such as retail or logistics.

A key mindset shift is treating cost not only as a defensive lever but also as a source of innovation. Savings from process improvements or procurement renegotiations should be reinvested in R&D, marketing, and digital acceleration—fueling sustainable growth.

This balance between austerity and reinvestment is a hallmark of outperforming organizations following a turnaround. As part of the capital allocation strategy, it brings new discipline and culture in evaluating costs and investments. The organization becomes nimble, efficient, collaborative, and growth-oriented by embedding cost ownership across departments, linking it to all C-level KPIs, and aligning budgets to strategy.

Deliverables:

- **Liquidity Resilience Framework**: A structured process for real-time cash monitoring, forecasting, and emergency funding readiness that ensures long-term solvency.
- **Long-Term Financial Modeling Dashboard**: Interactive dashboards tracking liquidity, debt, and capital costs to enable forward-looking financial planning and scenario testing.
- **Debt and Capital Structure Optimization Strategy**: A roadmap outlining refinancing tactics, leverage benchmarks, and funding sources aligned to growth and risk tolerance.

Embedding Operational Excellence

To ensure the improvements stick, the company must weave operational excellence into its DNA:

- **Standardization of Processes:** Document the optimized processes and standards developed during the turnaround so they become standard operating procedures (SOPs). For example, if the company implemented a new inventory management process during Phase 3 that reduced stockouts, Phase 4 ensures that the process is fully standardized across all departments or locations. Create checklists, manuals, and training modules for these SOPs. New employee onboarding should include training on these "new way of working" processes. The idea is to prevent regression.

Without documentation and training, old habits may resurface, or new team members might not be aware of the improved methods. Some companies pursue *certifications*, such as ISO 9001 for quality and ISO 55000 for asset management, to institutionalize process discipline and signal external parties that operational excellence is maintained. This also involves internal audits or assessments at regular intervals to verify that teams continue to follow the improved processes. Something I prefer to conduct mid-year is a self-assessment, so as not to confuse the team and bring the pressure of an internal audit.

- **Continuous Improvement Programs:** Establish a formal *Continuous Improvement (CI)*. This could be an office or a set of routines where employees regularly identify and implement incremental improvements, communicating them to top management through various channels, as well as receiving the usual reward associated with generating ideas and innovations. For instance, form quality circles or process excellence teams that meet monthly to discuss potential improvements, even after the turnaround projects are officially "done." Implement mechanisms for employees to submit improvement suggestions year-round (like a digital suggestion box or the CEO's email) and reward the best ideas. The goal is to maintain the momentum of positive change. Companies might adopt methodologies, such as *Six Sigma,* for ongoing projects to reduce defects and variability, or *Lean* initiatives to eliminate waste continuously. A tangible element could be holding an annual "Improvement Week" where teams showcase process enhancements they made and share them across the organization. By making CI a norm, the organization becomes self-correcting. Minor issues get addressed before they snowball into big problems. In our AC manufacturing case example, after achieving initial improvements, the company established an in-house "continuous improvement team" to drive ongoing efficiency gains, ensuring that the pursuit of excellence didn't end.

- **Metrics and Incentives Aligned to Excellence:** Revise KPIs and incentive systems to sustain focus on performance. For example, if the company has historically measured only financial outcomes, consider adding operational and organizational KPIs, such as cycle time, uptime, customer satisfaction, employee satisfaction, and turnover, to the executive scorecard so that maintaining the operational improvements remains a top priority for management. Tie some bonuses or raises to hitting these operational targets, not just short-term profit. The logic is to discourage shortcuts that may boost profit in the short term but undermine quality or efficiency in the long run. Also, publicize performance, such as plant efficiency rankings or customer service ratings by store, to instill a sense of competitive pride in excellence. When everyone knows that excellence is expected and rewarded, they are more likely to uphold the high standards that have been achieved. Essentially, bake operational excellence into the performance management of the company.

Building an Agile Supply Chain

i. Establish multiple sourcing strategies to reduce supplier dependency.

Supply chain resilience is a critical pillar of sustainability. After a turnaround, companies must move away from single-source dependencies that leave them vulnerable to disruptions. Multiple sourcing strategies, such as dual sourcing, regional diversification, or nearshoring, reduce operational risk while improving bargaining power. Strategic supplier segmentation can identify which relationships are critical, which can be replaced, and which are candidates for consolidation. Procurement teams should develop a "supplier health dashboard" to monitor supplier risk exposure and build contingency sourcing plans.

ii. Improve demand forecasting models to align production with sales trends.

An agile supply chain requires accurate, real-time forecasting. Using historical sales data, seasonality, and external market indicators, companies should deploy predictive analytics tools—powered by machine learning—to fine-tune their demand forecasts. Improved forecasting helps

Phase 4: Sustainability and Growth

optimize inventory levels, avoid stockouts or overproduction, and minimize working capital tied up in unsold goods. These models should be integrated across departments—from finance to operations to sales—for cross-functional visibility and coordination.

iii. Integrate sustainability initiatives (e.g., waste reduction, energy efficiency) into operations.

Modern supply chains must go beyond efficiency—they must be responsible. Organizations should conduct regular audits of their operations to identify excess waste, energy inefficiencies, and environmental impact. This aligns with the direction the Kingdom is heading as outlined in its Saudi Green Initiative. Lean tools, such as value stream mapping, can identify unnecessary steps, overprocessing, and excessive transport. Simultaneously, investments in renewable energy, fleet optimization, and recyclable packaging can reduce emissions while meeting ESG mandates. By aligning sustainability with supply chain agility, companies build operational credibility and long-term cost competitiveness.

Customer-Centric Performance Metrics

i. Implement Net Promoter Score (NPS) tracking to measure customer satisfaction (this is applicable more to large organizations).

Post-turnaround, customer experience becomes a key differentiator. NPS is a proven metric that captures how likely customers are to recommend the company. High scores correlate with loyalty and revenue retention, while low scores indicate dissatisfaction or a higher risk of churn. NPS should be embedded across customer segments, tracked over time, linked to operational improvements, and correlated with the entire life cycle of products and services to drive insights. Frontline staff should receive NPS-driven feedback to adjust service delivery in real time. However, a more intimate approach to feedback is recommended in organizations that deal with smaller numbers of clients. It fosters strong relationships with clients, ensuring immediate feedback and reducing the risk of client loss.

ii. Automate customer feedback loops to identify opportunities for service improvement.

Manually collected customer feedback is slow and reactive. Automating feedback through surveys, in-app prompts, and post-service follow-ups enables companies to collect timely data and quickly identify pain points. AI-powered sentiment analysis can scan written responses and customer support logs to flag emerging issues. A cross-functional "customer committee" should be established to review this data regularly and assign ownership for corrective actions and innovative ideas.

iii. Use AI-driven dynamic pricing models to optimize revenue and margins.

Static pricing leaves margin on the table. AI-driven dynamic pricing tools analyze competitor activity, demand signals, and inventory levels to recommend optimal prices. These models allow companies to protect margins while responding to market conditions in real time and minimize dead-weight loss between demand and supply in KSA due to subsidies and other practices (such as VAT differences in the region). In B2B, they can also customize pricing per customer based on volume, loyalty, or payment terms. Integrating pricing intelligence with CRM systems ensures alignment between marketing, sales, and revenue management.

Deliverables:

- **Lean Transformation Roadmap:** a tactical plan outlining waste elimination, process simplification, and ESG integration across the value chain to enhance long-term operational efficiency
- **Agile Supply Chain Playbook:** a documented framework with sourcing diversification strategies, demand planning models, and contingency logistics protocols to ensure supply continuity and responsiveness
- **Customer Experience Enhancement Strategy:** a strategic action plan integrating NPS tracking, automated feedback systems, and AI-powered pricing models to drive satisfaction, loyalty, and margin growth

Phase 4: Sustainability and Growth

Long-Term Financial Planning

With immediate financial crises resolved, Phase 4 shifts to prudent long-term financial management:

I. Multi-Year Financial Projections and Capital Allocation Strategy: Develop rolling three to five-year financial projections that reflect the post-turnaround reality and growth aspirations. These projections should be realistic but ambitious, showing steady revenue growth, margin improvement, and healthy cash generation. They become a compass for the company's strategic planning. Additionally, devise a capital allocation strategy: how will profits be used now that the company is likely to return to profitability? For example, decide on a target leverage ratio and use excess cash to pay down any remaining high-cost debt to maintain a strong balance sheet (a lesson learned from the distress). Alternatively, set priorities for reinvestment (a certain percentage of profits into R&D or expansion). This long-term view reassures investors and creditors that the company won't revert to poor financial habits. At *Events Investment Fund,* we developed a capital allocation strategy that defined everything, from which projects to consider to what investment threshold to apply, when to pay dividends, when to capitalize them, when to use debt, and for what. This helped us reduce capital requirements for growth from shareholders by 40 percent and brought a clear mindset to all leadership and the team. Phase 4 should institutionalize such lessons in its financial planning.

II. Governance for Financial Sustainability: Strengthen financial governance to prevent issues that may have led to the original distress. This can include more rigorous budgeting processes, quarterly strategy reviews, and involving the board more deeply in overseeing strategy execution. Perhaps establish a permanent *Risk and Compliance Committee* at the board level (if not already in place) to continuously monitor financial and operational risks. Also, adopt or enhance *financial transparency practices*. For instance, produce a detailed annual business performance review (one of the deliverables from Phase 4) and share key insights with employees and investors.

The idea is to create an environment with *no surprises* in financial results because issues are identified early and addressed. Consider adopting some elements of Zero-Based Budgeting (ZBB) for a couple of years, forcing every expense to be justified from scratch annually. This can prevent cost creep. By Phase 4, the mindset should shift from short-term survival to long-term value creation, but with a cautious eye that doesn't allow reckless spending or unchecked growth plans.

III. Investment in Growth and Innovation: On the financial side, plan for funding growth initiatives. Now that the business is stable, Phase 4 might involve raising new capital (equity or debt). However, this time, it is for *offensive purposes*, e.g., funding a strategic acquisition or a major new product development, rather than to cover losses. As part of the Capital Allocation Strategy section, the criteria for such investments are to ensure they meet return thresholds and align with the strategy. The company could even consider restoring shareholder returns if applicable (like resuming dividends or share buybacks), but balanced against reinvestment needs. Communicating this capital strategy clearly to shareholders will be integral to setting expectations. Essentially, long-term financial planning involves using healthier finances as a catalyst for growth while safeguarding the company's financial stability.

Leadership Development and Organizational Agility

i. Strengthening Leadership and Decision-Making

A turnaround cannot sustain itself unless supported by strong, resilient leadership. Following the turnaround, a KSA organization must institutionalize decision-making rhythms, data-informed management, and leadership development programs that enhance internal bench strength. Having seen many leaders run organizations in KSA with a centralized structure at the top—sometimes due to a lack of talent around them—this phase is the most critical to a long-sustaining turnaround.

Establishing a monthly or quarterly strategy review cadence—not just annual reviews—is mandatory to ensure continuous alignment between operations and strategic priorities. These reviews should be outcome-

Phase 4: Sustainability and Growth

focused, reviewing KPIs, strategic initiatives, risk status, and emerging trends. In high-change environments, quarterly reviews are often insufficient; leading companies adopt monthly "strategy sprints" where teams iterate on progress and recalibrate their strategies. This is imperative in the early days after the turnaround and before the new culture is deeply ingrained as part of the new organization.

Training the leadership team in data-driven decision-making is paramount in a world ruled by data, where leaders are becoming increasingly younger and less experienced. Many legacy managers rely on instinct or hierarchy rather than insight. A strong decision-making culture begins by training teams on tools such as scenario modeling, financial dashboards, and operational analytics while ensuring access to high-quality data. Embedding cross-functional data access platforms reduces dependency on manual reporting and empowers faster action.

Equally important is building the next generation of KSA leadership through succession pipelines. This involves identifying high-potential employees across departments, exposing them to mission-critical projects, empowering them, and allowing them to make mistakes while providing them (or pairing them with) strong leadership to mentor them during this process. A formal leadership development program can include executive coaching, mentorship programs, rotational roles, and action-learning projects tied to growth or transformation initiatives.

Post-turnaround, the company must have competent leadership and a resilient decision-making structure built on routines, facts, and forward-looking talent.

ii. Creating a Culture of Performance & Accountability

The cultural reset that starts in a turnaround must evolve into a high-performance culture that sustains momentum. At the core, this is building a system where every team member connects their performance to enterprise outcomes. At one of the companies I handled, I developed two different weighting systems for the company employees' KPIs responsibilities: One was for the C-level where their KPIs were linked to 60–70 percent of the organization achieving its targets, and 30–40 percent was linked to their individual KPIs (not to forget that they also were behaviorally assessed during the year at least three times). The second system was designed for department-level individuals, and 30–40 percent of their KPIs were linked to the overall organization targets. This created a system of accountability for the entire organization, including colleagues from other departments and employees, who were forced to collaborate.

Each company is different, obviously, but KPIs should not just measure output. They should also include quality, timeliness, and impact. Another example in a sales department is tracking margin quality or the retention rate of acquired customers beyond just meeting quota. Incentives, whether financial or recognition-based, should reward measurable contributions, not tenure.

Cross-functional collaboration is another essential lever of agility. Organizations in transformation and startups often face "restructuring fatigue" or "near-burnout" with silos reemerging. Leaders must create opportunities for team-based success, such as shared KPIs across functions, co-led initiatives, or joint problem-solving teams. Implementing a "no hand-off" culture (where no one passes on problems without owning outcomes) fosters true accountability.

Additionally, embed employee-led innovation programs. Invite teams to suggest and pilot process improvements or customer experience upgrades, such as resolving problems for the company, and form cross-functional teams around such initiatives. Support this with small budgets or rewards for winners, mentorship, and recognition. Employees who are empowered to contribute develop ownership—not just compliance.

Ultimately, leadership behaviors reinforce this culture, characterized by transparency, follow-through, and mutual accountability. It must become unacceptable to miss targets without discussion, just as proposing solutions proactively is expected.

iii. Retention and Talent Growth Strategies

In the post-turnaround phase, retaining high performers and building future talent pipelines becomes mission-critical. Companies that ignore this in KSA, which has a market lacking a large pool of talent, often see

Phase 4: Sustainability and Growth

top talent depart just when stability is achieved, leaving gaps in execution and innovation.

First, implement competency-based workforce planning. Map roles not only by titles and job descriptions but by the competencies they require—strategic thinking, digital fluency, customer centricity, and more. Use this to assess workforce fit, uncover skill gaps, and direct development efforts.

Performance-based rewards are crucial in bringing all the changes made to tie up what I call the "four boxes around" strategy. Offering stock options, phantom shares, or performance bonuses aligned to long-term goals (e.g., three-year EBITDA targets) ties employee success to enterprise value creation. It also conveys that the company now operates with shared accountability and upside, but those can also go wrong. Suppose you ask your employees to innovate and spend time working together to develop ideas and solutions, and your reward system is linked to numbers and current operational KPIs. Then, no culture of innovation can be sustained.

Partner with top universities, think tanks, and professional institutes to maintain a steady influx of future talent. Establish intern and management trainee pipelines for early-career talent, as well as joint research programs or innovation labs for more senior recruitment. This strengthens your brand as an employer of choice and signals to the market that you are a growth-minded organization that cares about employees' health (e.g., establishing a gym or exercise room, providing nutritious food, or offering a life coach to work with your employees). When creating a recruitment journey like Road to XYZ, ensure that potential candidates become so excited that even if you pay less than others, they will value your culture and environment more highly than those of your competitors. Whatever it is, and whatever budget you have, create something special to retain your top talent.

Finally, integrate career path visibility and internal mobility programs. Let employees see how they can grow within the company. When staff believe they can build a future within the organization, their loyalty and engagement rise—turning good talent into enduring assets.

Deliverables:

i. **Leadership Succession Planning Guide:** a structured roadmap identifying future leaders, development plans, and readiness levels to ensure sustainable leadership continuity.
ii. **Organizational Agility Framework:** a blueprint outlining cross-functional collaboration models, rapid decision-making practices, and performance alignment systems for a more adaptive workforce.
iii. **KPI-Based Employee Incentive Plan:** a transparent, tiered incentive structure linking individual and team KPIs to recognition and reward mechanisms, reinforcing high performance and accountability.

Digital Transformation and Technology Adoption

Innovation and Market Expansion Strategies

With a solid foundation, the company looks outward again for opportunities:

i. **New Product/Service Development:** Leverage the breathing room gained to *reignite innovation*. If R&D were cut during the crisis, Phase 4 would see its prudent restoration in areas with high potential. Establish a pipeline of new products or service improvements informed by the latest market trends and customer feedback (which the company has hopefully attuned to again). For example, if the turnaround company is a tech firm, Phase 4 might involve catching up on a missed tech trend, such as launching a cloud-based version of their software, as the market has shifted in that direction. If it's a manufacturer, perhaps developing an eco-friendly product line would be beneficial if sustainability is a growing demand. Implement an innovation framework, such as allocating a percentage of revenue to R&D, establishing cross-functional innovation teams, and possibly partnering with external entities (startups, universities) to co-develop new offerings. The goal is to ensure the company doesn't become stagnant; it should be driving forward with competitive offerings that fuel growth.

Phase 4: Sustainability and Growth

At one of the companies I was leading, I launched a cross-functional team to compete for innovating and finding creative ideas for three topics, such as "How can we use blockchain technologies in our assets?" "How can we use digital twins and the metaverse?" or "How do we become an organization of innovators and trendsetters?" It was one of the most creative outcomes I have ever seen from the team there. That underscores how a turnaround can serve as a platform for innovation-led expansion.

ii. Market Expansion and Customer Growth: Phase 4 might involve re-entering markets that were previously exited or entering new geographies or segments now that the core is strong. Develop a strategic marketing plan for expansion, whether through opening new distribution channels, targeting new customer demographics, or even acquisitions to gain market access. A service company could consider expanding its offerings or opening branches in new regions. A manufacturer might look to export to new markets or diversify into adjacent product categories. These moves should be data-driven: use the improved market intelligence capabilities developed during the turnaround to pinpoint where growth is most feasible and profitable. Also, capitalize on the revitalized brand reputation that should come from a successful turnaround. Communicate to the market that the company is back and better than before. In Phase 4, our company should also look at scaling its reach.

iii. Digital Transformation and Adaptation: In modern turnarounds, Phase 4 often involves ensuring the company is future-ready from a technology perspective. If not already addressed, implement the remaining aspects of *digital transformation*, such as e-commerce channels, AI-driven data analytics capabilities, or automation, to enhance competitiveness. This ties back to innovation but is specifically about modernizing business models. The company should examine its customer journey and operations to identify last-mile tech upgrades that can yield growth or efficiency. Maybe invest in a CRM to personalize marketing (leading to higher customer retention) or develop an online platform if historically brick-and-mortar. Being tech-forward is becoming the norm in sustaining success. For example, many companies that turned around in the 2010s attributed their sustained success to embracing digital: a retailer might survive bankruptcy and then thrive by pivoting strongly to online sales. Thus, Phase 4 in the AI world is incomplete without a technology roadmap to ensure the company doesn't fall behind again, especially as AI adoption drives rapid industry evolution and renders old ways obsolete.

Deliverables:

i. **IT Roadmap with Cybersecurity Strategy:** a comprehensive plan outlining the company's long-term digital infrastructure upgrades, including system integrations, cloud migration, and data security protocols. This roadmap ensures the business remains resilient, scalable, and protected against growing cybersecurity threats as it modernizes.
ii. **AI-Powered Sales and Marketing Transformation Plan:** a targeted strategy to embed AI capabilities in customer segmentation, personalization, and campaign performance tracking. This initiative helps drive predictive insights, increase conversion rates, and automate decision-making for scalable growth in customer acquisition and retention.
iii. **Industry 4.0 Manufacturing Integration Framework:** a blueprint for implementing innovative factory technologies, including IoT, digital twins, and automation, to enhance operational visibility and productivity. This ensures manufacturing operations become more agile, cost-efficient, and innovation-driven, securing long-term competitiveness in the post-turnaround era.

Governance, Compliance, and Risk Management

i. Strengthening Corporate Governance

Robust governance ensures the company not only sustains its turnaround but also evolves into a high-performing, investor-trusted organization. A dedicated risk and compliance committee reporting directly to the board institutionalizes oversight and embeds risk awareness into decision-making. This committee should meet quarterly, include independent direc-

Phase 4: Sustainability and Growth

tors, and have clear mandates on financial integrity, legal compliance, and strategic risk exposure.

Financial transparency is paramount. Companies must publish timely and accurate financial statements that align with international standards (e.g., GAAP). Transparency builds investor confidence, supports better capital access, and holds management accountable. This also includes clear disclosures of board activity, executive remuneration, and risk exposure in shareholder communications.

I personally like to create multiple committees that are carefully structured and well-defined. A magic number for top-performing companies should be eight to nine committees between the board and management committees. Some committees are more important than others, such as the SteerCo, Capital Allocation Committee, Operational Risk Committee, and Hiring and Culture Committee. The board and leadership must be cautious in developing governance, engaging with and assessing committee members, and consistently communicating governance issues as they arise.

Also, annual independent and internal audits help reinforce credibility, flag internal control gaps, and assure stakeholders. These audits should go beyond financial reviews to cover operational compliance, cybersecurity, ESG performance, and governance maturity. The audit firm's findings should be presented directly to the board, not just to management.

Post-turnaround companies often struggle with the temptation to return to centralized, opaque decision-making. Reinforcing checks and balances prevents relapse. Strong governance isn't bureaucracy, as you frequently started to see in KSA. It's a value multiplier. It is NOT just "*checks and balances*," as some very influential people in KSA say. At its core, it is a governance framework that fosters transparency, facilitates a smooth decision-making process, ensures accountability to both the board and employees, and encourages collaboration.

ii. Regulatory and Compliance Enhancement

Sustained performance requires continuous compliance with both local regulations (Labor, Zakat, cybersecurity) and global standards for those dealing with broader regional and international markets (data privacy, environmental laws, anti-bribery). To achieve this, a compliance dashboard should be implemented across all departments, assigning ownership and timelines to every obligation. This tool should be updated monthly and tracked by the compliance officer or legal team.

The company should also develop an integrated ESG strategy to meet investor expectations and future-proof the business. ESG performance impacts brand reputation, access to capital, employee pride, and customer loyalty, especially in regulated or consumer-facing industries.

ESG policies should align with local and international frameworks (e.g., SGI, UN SDGs, SASB, GRI) and encompass areas such as carbon footprint, workforce diversity, and ethical supply chain practices. This signals to investors that the company operates responsibly and strategically.

Finally, compliance cannot be siloed—it must be embedded into the culture, supported by training, leadership commitment, and audit trails.

iii. Risk Monitoring and Crisis Preparedness

Turnarounds often collapse post-recovery due to unanticipated disruptions. At this stage, we have already created and thought of all the possible ways we can fail. Then, we identified the risks and mitigation plans. However, we still need to have an agile and flexible mindset to effectively monitor and manage risks. Establishing real-time risk dashboards gives leadership visibility into early warning indicators across operational, financial, and reputational domains. Some examples include rising customer complaints, falling inventory turns, or unusual IT access logs—all of which should trigger alerts.

Every primary function — finance, operations, HR, and IT — must maintain a live risk register, which is reviewed on a weekly or monthly basis. Assign "risk owners" who are accountable for monitoring and mitigation.

Complement this with robust Business Continuity Plans (BCPs). These should detail responses for various crises: cyberattacks, construction damages, artist accidents, or supplier failures. Each BCP should define roles, recovery steps, timelines, and communication protocols.

Phase 4: Sustainability and Growth

What distinguishes great companies is not their avoidance of crisis but their anticipation, speed, and structure in managing one. Embedding this mindset ensures that the momentum built in the turnaround isn't lost when external shocks occur.

Deliverables:

- **Corporate Governance and Board Structure Optimization Plan:** A comprehensive framework defining board composition, committee roles, and governance best practices to ensure long-term accountability and strategic oversight
- **Compliance Risk Assessment Framework:** A tool to map legal and regulatory obligations, assign ownership, and monitor real-time adherence across departments
- **Business Continuity and Crisis Response Strategy:** A playbook detailing roles, actions, and timelines for responding to financial, operational, or reputational crises, ensuring minimal disruption during unforeseen events

Growth Acceleration and Market Expansion

i. Geographic and Product Expansion

After stabilization, the company must pivot from preservation to growth. Geographic expansion involves entering new markets—domestic or international—where demand aligns with the company's capabilities. This requires conducting market feasibility studies, assessing regulatory risks, and building scalable go-to-market strategies.

Expansion should be strategic, not opportunistic. Companies must prioritize geographies with clear value potential (e.g., underserved regions, high-growth markets, or proximity to strategic partners) and execute with a controlled launch strategy (e.g., pilot region, phased rollout). Local knowledge is crucial in expansion. Some industries, such as real estate, banking, and financial management, require strategic partnerships with local/regional partners.

Simultaneously, product line extensions are critical. Companies can identify adjacent product categories or enhancements that fulfill unmet needs by analyzing customer behavior, feedback, and purchasing trends, as well as identifying customers' lifetime value. For example, a company with a successful physical product might launch a digital extension or bundled services to boost customer lifetime value.

Growth must be resource-aligned with no overextension and meet capital allocation strategy requirements. Expansion plans should be tied to financial scenarios, operational capacity, and clear success metrics.

ii. Strategic Partnerships and M&A Readiness

Post-turnaround companies often become attractive acquisition targets or, conversely, are well-positioned to make strategic acquisitions. Either way, M&A readiness must be baked into the growth strategy.

This entails maintaining clean books, documented systems, and scalable operations. Strategic partnerships like JVs or distribution alliances can accelerate market penetration, enable access to IP or supply chains, and reduce capital risk.

The company should identify potential M&A targets or partners aligned with its long-term goals and capital allocation strategy. A framework for screening, evaluating, and integrating acquisitions must be developed as part of the capital allocation strategy and in advance to avoid post-deal chaos. Likewise, integration plans should include cultural fit assessments, synergy targets, and post-deal communication protocols.

Growth through partnerships or M&A should never dilute the operational focus. Instead, it should compound existing momentum.

iii. Capital Allocation for Sustainable Growth

Having capital is one thing; deploying it wisely is another. A capital allocation strategy ensures that every dollar invested aligns with the company's long-term strategic objectives and produces measurable returns.

Management must define a capital deployment philosophy: specifying what percentage goes to R&D, new markets, and infrastructure; when to

Phase 4: Sustainability and Growth

use debt and when to avoid it; and when to distribute dividends. Establishing a Capital Allocation Committee can bring objectivity and data-driven rigor to major funding decisions.

Companies must balance short-term profit-taking (e.g., paying down debt) with long-term reinvestment (e.g., product innovation, tech upgrades). Capital allocation should be reviewed quarterly, with scenario planning to test the impact of large investments under different economic conditions.

An optimized capital strategy keeps the company agile, competitive, and focused, positioning it to recover and lead.

Deliverables:

- **Market Expansion and Internationalization Plan:** A roadmap for entering new markets and launching new products, complete with feasibility analysis, execution milestones, and KPIs
- **M&A Integration Framework:** A structured process for identifying, evaluating, and integrating acquisition targets or joint venture partners to accelerate strategic growth
- **Long-Term Capital Allocation Strategy:** A governance-backed approach for deploying capital across R&D, operations, and growth, aligned with financial returns and strategic objectives

Improvement and Agility Frameworks

To avoid future decline, the company must remain agile and continuously improve:

> **i. Agility in Strategy and Operations:** Introduce frameworks that allow the company to *sense and respond to changes quickly*. This could include adopting an agile strategic planning process. Instead of static annual plans, move to rolling quarterly strategic updates, allowing the company to pivot if market conditions change. Operationally, perhaps implement agile project management in product development (sprints, rapid prototyping in the age of AI) to keep innovation cycles fast. The organization should preserve the "scrappiness" it had during the turnaround—the ability to

mobilize cross-functional teams to tackle challenges, even when times are good. I would institutionalize this by periodically running "war games" or scenario planning exercises to test their readiness for various situations, such as a sudden commodity price spike or a competitor's introduction of a new disruptive product.

ii. By doing so, they keep the team's problem-solving muscles in shape. This ensures the *problem-solving culture* nurtured during a crisis is not lost to complacency. Celebrate not just the final results but also the adaptive responses. For example, once, I asked my development team to monitor cement prices and their impact on our project before we started and to run a scenario analysis on cost in case of price changes. Based on that, we identified a strategy to secure and hedge our needs for specific projects. This agility needed to be recognized because it helped the team to remain agile and adapt quickly to different scenarios.

iii. Benchmarking and External Orientation: Maintain a habit of *external benchmarking* even in good times. Phase 4 companies should regularly compare themselves against industry bests and emerging players. This prevents the inward-looking complacency that sometimes creeps in after a post-turnaround success. I like to set up a semiannual benchmarking review as part of a strategy to look at new entrants, technological trends, and customer preference shifts. If any metric indicates that the company is slipping relative to competitors, initiate a project (with that continuous improvement mindset) to address it.

iv. Additionally, engage in industry forums and maintain open dialogue with customers and suppliers. An external focus ensures the company stays ahead of the curve. One can recall how IBM, after its 90s turnaround, kept reinventing itself through the 2000s by staying attuned to market changes (moving into services, then into cloud and AI). It's that kind of vigilance that Phase 4 should embed as a structural component.

v. Knowledge Retention and Handover: External experts or special teams are often involved during a turnaround. Phase 4 should ensure that all that *knowledge is captured and transferred* to the permanent organization. If

Phase 4: Sustainability and Growth

consultants led many initiatives, their insights and documentation should be retained, and internal people should be trained to continue the work. The same applies to systems—ensure that all new systems and processes have multiple people capable of running them. Avoid key-man risk: no single individual, such as the CRO or a superstar project manager, should hold critical know-how without backup. By the end of Phase 4, the company should be able to operate and continuously improve *independently* of any turnaround-specific resources. This often means formal training programs and manuals written by those who led Phase 3 projects, now handed off to line managers. A smooth transition here marks the difference between a one-time turnaround and a permanently enhanced organization.

Psychological Considerations in Phase 4 (Sustainability and Growth)

By Phase 4, the organizational mindset should shift from caution to *confidence*, but managing this shift carefully is necessary. After a successful turnaround, employees may feel a mix of relief, pride, and even lingering caution: "We never want to go through that again." Psychologically, leadership should reinforce a sense of *achievement*. Recognize how far the company has come and celebrate the collective effort. This could be done via company-wide events or rewards. Some companies give all staff a bonus or extra time off when major turnaround milestones are hit as a "thank-you" for perseverance. Such gestures strengthen loyalty and validate the hard work.

However, there's also a risk of *complacency* setting in once things improve. To guard against this, leaders must instill the idea that "turnaround is a journey, not a destination." Emphasize that continuous improvement is now part of the job, not an extraordinary project. Sometimes, bringing in *new talent* at this stage (if it hasn't already been done) can infuse fresh energy and prevent groupthink within the team. New hires who weren't in crisis mode might question, "Why do we do things this way?" Or a new hire from a different industry might ask, "Why do you do the compressor testing for leakage again before AC box assembly?" and push further improvements. That healthy questioning should be encouraged rather than shut down with "because that's how we survived." In other words, the psychology should shift from survival mode to a *growth mindset*.

Another consideration is reconciling the experiences of the turnaround. The culture likely changed under stress. Perhaps it became more top-down and intense to push changes through. In Phase 4, the company can ease back into a more *participative and developmental culture* now that the immediate danger is over. This means empowering employees more, encouraging calculated risk-taking for innovation, and focusing on personal development and career growth, which might have been deprioritized during the crisis. People will appreciate the return of opportunities (promotions, training, etc.), which boosts morale and forward-looking optimism.

It's also worthwhile to *memorialize lessons learned* to shape the organizational memory. Conduct postmortem reviews: what did we learn about our markets, processes, and culture from this turnaround? A document or internal case study should be included in onboarding new employees, such as "This is who we are: a company that went through tough times and emerged stronger. This is how we did it." This narrative can be powerful in strengthening organizational identity and cohesion. Employees often develop camaraderie (fellowship) from having endured a turnaround. Phase 4 should harness that bond to build a strong culture.

Finally, acknowledge any remaining anxieties. Some may worry, "What if we slip again?" Leaders should address this by highlighting the safeguards in place, such as improved systems and monitoring, while maintaining approachability. If anyone sees warning signs, they should speak up. Ensure that an open communication culture will continue. The willingness to discuss problems early is one of the greatest cultural assets from a turnaround and must be preserved. By Phase 4, ideally, the predominant emotion in the organization is *confidence*: confidence grounded in the knowledge that "we overcame adversity by working together, and we have the tools to keep succeeding." Maintaining that confident yet vigilant mindset ensures the company's future is bright and secure.

Final Deliverables of Phase 4: By the conclusion of Phase 4, a few key

Phase 4: Sustainability and Growth

outputs signal the formal end of the turnaround program and the handoff to "business-as-usual" growth mode:

1. Turnaround Sustainability Report: a comprehensive report documenting all changes made, results achieved, and how the company will continue to uphold improvements. This report serves as both an internal reference and an external communication tool to investors, boards, and banks. It should detail financial improvements (e.g., debt reduced from X to Y, margins increased from A percent to B percent), operational gains (productivity metrics, quality stats), and market outcomes (market share, customer feedback improvements). More importantly, it outlines the *ongoing governance*. For instance, "We have established a permanent Strategy Committee and Continuous Improvement team to monitor performance and drive future initiatives." It might include a section on "lessons learned" and recommendations for the future to avoid past pitfalls (e.g., avoiding over-leveraging for growth and maintaining a conservative debt-to-equity below X). Essentially, this report is the capstone, confirming that *the turnaround delivered value, and here's how we'll ensure the company remains healthy*. It provides closure and accountability, demonstrating to stakeholders that their support paid off with tangible outcomes.

2. Annual Business Performance Review Process: One deliverable is the institution of a robust annual (or ongoing) performance review mechanism. Unlike a one-time report, this is about creating a *process*. For example, a yearly strategic planning and budgeting cycle should incorporate the rigorous analysis used in the turnaround. The deliverable could be described as a framework document or calendar: "Each year, in Q3, the company will undertake a full review of financial and operational performance, benchmark against peers, and update a three-year strategic plan." It ensures that the discipline of the turnaround becomes routine.

The turnaround office can facilitate the first review post-turnaround to transition knowledge to normal management. This process might also involve scenario planning for downside cases, effectively keeping the organization's crisis management skills sharp (but hopefully not needed). By formalizing this, the company acknowledges that sustaining success is an ongoing effort, not a one-time project.

3. Risk Management and Crisis Response Playbook: As a final deliverable, the team should compile a *Risk Management and Crisis Response Playbook*. This guides the organization in handling future shocks, essentially institutionalizing what was learned. It would include risk monitoring processes (maybe an outline of key risk indicators to watch regularly, my favorite being leading indicators), predefined action plans for specific scenarios (like a checklist for responding to a sudden liquidity crunch or supply chain interruption or as remote as some companies think like the collapse of a ceiling), and roles/responsibilities in a crisis (who forms the war room, etc.). Having this playbook means if early warning signs ever appear again, the company won't hesitate or scramble—it will have a tested approach ready, improving resilience. Think of it as the "break glass in case of emergency" manual drawn from the turnaround experience. Creating it as a deliverable forces the team to reflect on what measures worked and codify them for future reference. This also reassures stakeholders (especially lenders and investors) that the company is better prepared. For example, a company might include in this playbook the thirteen-week cash flow model template used, communication protocols for crisis management, such as how often to update the board or employees, and contingency funding sources identified during the turnaround. This final deliverable means the legacy of the turnaround is a permanently more vigilant and resilient enterprise.

Key Takeaways from Phase 4: By now, the turnaround journey has imparted crucial lessons:

- **Sustainability = Continuous Evolution:** The end of a turnaround isn't a return to stasis but the start of constant, proactive improvement. Companies that successfully turn around understand that *standing still means falling behind*. They embed mechanisms to keep evolving, which is why *continuous growth and innovation* are the accurate measures of a sustainable turnaround.

- **Resilience Through Risk Management:** A major insight is that building buffers and *planning for risks* in good times can prevent future crises. Whether maintaining strong cash reserves, diversifying revenue streams, or having a robust growth and crisis playbook like this, the companies that endure have woven resilience into their strategy. As noted, those that embed turnaround best practices into their DNA outperform their peers in the long term because they can *weather storms better and respond faster.*

• **Culture is King for Long-Term Success:** Perhaps the most important takeaway is the power of culture, as exemplified by the famous headline "Culture eats strategy for breakfast." A culture that values accountability, fact-based decision-making, and agility, forged during the turnaround, will differentiate the company moving forward. It separates the long-term winners from those who merely had a temporary fix. A complacent culture with poor leadership can undo all structural fixes. In contrast, a high-performing culture grounded in strong values will continue to drive gains even in a stable environment.

AI Integration Across Turnaround Phases

AI is becoming a reality in everyday life, but not every company should integrate it without careful assessment and a well-thought-out plan. That said, the use and integration of AI in a turnaround situation must be used as enhancements to be included in all phases of the turnaround:

Assessment, Implementation, Execution, and Sustainability: A well-used technical assessment done through AI could potentially reduce the time of each phase by 40 percent, making the turnaround fast and potentially more concrete.

Phase 1: Assessment—AI for Business Model Evaluation

Purpose: assess AI's impact on the company's industry and business model viability.

- AI should be analyzed for competitive threats and opportunities. For example, retail companies must evaluate how AI-driven personalization transforms customer engagement. Services should assess the viability of using AI bots to enhance customers' experiences and add another layer to the interaction, making it more seamless and reducing additional frustration. Does it solve 80 percent of the customers' inquiries and get immediate feedback to roll out if it does not help? Manufacturers should assess whether *smart automation* can reduce inefficiencies.

- **AI Benchmarking Analysis:** Companies should compare their *AI adoption maturity* with that of industry leaders to identify areas for improvement. If competitors leverage *AI-driven cost optimization* but the company doesn't, it may struggle to compete.

Phase 2: Planning—AI-driven Cost Reduction and Revenue Growth

Purpose: Embed AI into the *turnaround plan* to reduce implementation time and drive cost efficiency and revenue growth.

- **Predictive AI Cost-Cutting:** AI-powered expense analytics can flag excessive spending patterns, while procurement AI optimizes supplier negotiation strategies.

- **AI-driven Market Strategy:** AI can segment customers dynamically and optimize pricing strategies based on real-time demand elasticity.

Phase 3: Implementation—AI-powered Execution and Process Optimization

Purpose: Utilize AI to streamline execution efficiency.

- **AI-Powered Risk Management:** AI-driven risk models can analyze financial, operational, and market risks dynamically.

- **Automated Workforce Productivity Monitoring:** AI-driven employee performance monitoring ensures accountability while optimizing workforce utilization.

Phase 4: Sustainability—AI for Continuous Improvement and Innovation

Purpose: Establish AI as a competitive advantage post-turnaround.

- **AI-Powered Business Intelligence:** AI should be integrated into ongoing performance monitoring to continuously optimize operations.

- **AI Innovation Pipeline:** Companies must establish a roadmap for *AI-driven innovation*, ensuring they don't fall behind their competitors after stabilizing.

Final Thoughts on the Complete Playbook

This four-phase turnaround playbook demonstrates that reviving a distressed company is a complex but achievable journey. It requires rigorous analysis, bold decision-making, and sensitive change management. Each phase builds logically on the previous: *Assessment* grounds the effort in facts. *Planning* charts the path. *Implementation* drives the change. *Sustainability* secures the future. Skipping or rushing any phase can undermine the whole effort.

One overarching insight is that *turnarounds are as much an art as a science*. The science lies in the data, analysis, and structured frameworks, such as those McKinsey or Bain would employ. The art lies in leading people from fear to hope, from old ways to new habits. A successful turnaround leader is much like a founder of a startup who must wear many hats: visionary, crisis manager, communicator, strategist, and cheerleader.

The playbook serves as a guide for organizations undergoing this process, but flexibility is key. Every company situation has unique elements (industry dynamics, competitive landscape, internal culture) that must be taken into consideration. Thus, while following best practices, constantly tailor and adjust the approach. Additionally, never underestimate the *power of quick wins* and storytelling. Early visible successes and a compelling narrative of "where we're headed" can create a virtuous cycle of buy-in and effort that pushes the turnaround forward against the odds.

Lastly, a completed turnaround is not just a return to normal but an opportunity to reach new heights. Many of the case studies referenced—from Apple to Marvel to Duet or AG&P—didn't just survive; they emerged stronger and often attained leadership positions in their industries after recovery. This playbook aspires to equip any turnaround CEO or team with the mindset and toolkit to achieve similar outcomes. By converting a crisis into a strategic reset, a company can fulfill the maxim: *"Never let a good crisis go to waste."* In doing so, what was once a failing enterprise can transform into a *future-ready, thriving business* positioned for long-term success.

Comparative Analysis: Turnaround Versus Startup

In closing, it's insightful to compare the journey of a turnaround leader with that of a startup, as both are involved in intensive change and building (or rebuilding) value from a low point:

- **Initial Conditions:** A startup begins from scratch—typically on a *small scale, with limited resources, cash flow crunch, but a blank canvas* unburdened by legacy. In contrast, a turnaround typically begins with a *legacy organization*—established assets, processes, and people, but also baggage of past failures and often a larger scale. A turnaround must unlearn or dismantle things (e.g., bad strategies and inefficient operations). In contrast, a startup must create everything new (strategy, operations), often with no established reputation or market presence. Paradoxically, both operate under resource constraints (startups due to lack of initial capital and cash flow limitations, turnarounds due to a crisis of capital and limited funding sources), which can spur creativity. As someone who did both, I can say that in a startup, you beg for resources and backing; in a turnaround, you slash to survive. Either way, you learn to do more with less and develop a skill to rally and motivate people around a common cause.

Final Thoughts on the Complete Playbook

- **Risk and Uncertainty:** Both startups and turnarounds face high uncertainty and risk of failure. Statistically, a high percentage of startups fail in their first few years, and similarly, many distressed turnarounds do not succeed. However, the nature of risks differs. *Startups* wrestle with market risk (Will customers adopt our new product?) and execution risk of building a viable business model from zero. *Turnarounds* deal more with organizational risk (Can we change entrenched behaviors?) and financial risk (Can we stave off creditors and stabilize our cash flow?). A startup's risk is often external—finding product-market fit—whereas a turnaround's risk is internal and external—fixing internal issues while convincing external stakeholders (customers, creditors) not to abandon ship. Both require a tolerance for ambiguity and a pivot-ready mentality. In a way, a turnaround team must reignite a *startup mindset* within a mature company—emphasizing speed, innovation, and a willingness to pivot—to navigate out of trouble.

- **Culture and Psychology:** Culturally, startups typically have enthusiasm and a growth mindset from day one. Everything is new. The team is building something they believe in. Although pressure exists, it's often positive pressure that creates and fosters growth. Turnarounds frequently start with a *culture of fear or defeat*. Employees have seen things go wrong, morale is low, and trust in management may be broken. The turnaround effort must transform this into a "can-do" culture, essentially refounding the company. In successful cases, treating the turnaround as a "rebirth" of the company helps instill entrepreneurial spirit as if it were a startup. Conversely, once the turnaround gains momentum, employees might feel even more bonded and proud than a startup team, as they have overcome adversity together. I like to say that *startups create culture, and turnarounds repair culture*: both are deeply concerned with culture-building, but one is proactive creation, and the other is fixing and transforming an existing culture.

- **Strategy Formation:** In a startup, strategy is hypothesis-driven and evolves quickly—there's freedom to try to pivot the business model until something sticks. In a turnaround, strategy is constrained by history. You have existing customers, products, and commitments; you can't pivot as freely without consequences. However, a turnaround often involves a refocusing strategy similar to a startup finding its focus: identifying a viable core business and shedding distractions is akin to a startup honing its MVP (minimum viable product) and core value proposition. The timeline pressures differ: startups feel the urgency to grow before their cash runs out or their competitors win, while turnarounds feel the urgency to shrink inefficiencies and return to profit before cash runs out or creditors enforce liquidation. In both, *speed is essential*, but the actions you take quickly differ.

- Startups: Iterate product and market fit
- Turnarounds: Implement cost cuts, drop unprofitable products, process fixes, and refocus

Interestingly, both often benefit from *small, cross-functional teams*. Tackling key issues, emphasizing that agility and teamwork are universal success factors, and creativity and collaboration are the only way forward for both.

• **Resource Acquisition:** Startups seek investment from VCs, angel investors, etc., selling a vision of future growth. Turnarounds may seek fresh capital or creditor leniency, selling a story of recovery and renewed stability. In essence, both need to inspire confidence in stakeholders about a future that's better than the present. A charismatic founder might secure funding for a dream; a credible turnaround CEO secures backing on a solid plan. Both often require convincing skeptics: for startups, that the idea can be successful, and for turnarounds, that the company can change. The communications in both cases need to be compelling and evidence-based, albeit with different narratives (disruptive innovation versus disciplined transformation).

• **Outcome and Success Measures:** A startup's success is typically measured by growth, such as user acquisition, revenue ramp,

Final Thoughts on the Complete Playbook

market traction, and culminating in profitability (though often later). A turnaround's success is measured by improvement, such as halting losses, returning to profitability, restoring stakeholder confidence, and then growth. Startups aim to go from 0 to 1 (create something new), and turnarounds aim to go from -1 back to 0 and beyond (fix and then grow). In both journeys, reaching a stable and profitable business model is the ultimate goal. A commonality is that *both can lead to exponential success if done correctly*. A successful startup can become a billion-dollar business; a successful turnaround can transform a failing giant into a leader again. For example, Apple's startup phase and, later, its turnaround propelled it to become the world's most valuable company. In both phases, Steve Jobs led as an entrepreneur at heart. Thus, while starting points differ, the endgame converges: a robust, sustainable company delivering value to customers and stakeholders.

Conclusion of Comparison: A startup is about creation and growth in the face of uncertainty, whereas a turnaround is about reinvention and recovery under distress. They share the need for visionary leadership (Think Steve again!), relentless execution, and an aligned team willing to go through fire for a vision. Each can learn from the other: startups can adopt some turnaround discipline (focusing on cash flows and profitability early on rather than just growth at any cost), and turnarounds can adopt startup dynamism (innovating and pivoting boldly, not just cutting). Both paths are challenging but incredibly rewarding. Building something new or saving something great are both noble business endeavors. The playbook I've detailed, while focused on turnarounds, carries many principles (customer focus, agility, culture shaping) that are equally applicable to the startup context, underlining that at the heart of both is **sound management and inspired leadership** and having done both, I reiterate, it is an ART, not a science.

Case Studies

CASE STUDY 1: PRIVATE EQUITY REAL ESTATE FUND "PEREF" (THE NAME IS NOT DISCLOSED FOR CONFIDENTIALITY PURPOSES.)

Applying the Turnaround Playbook in a Startup Fund/ Company Context

Initial Context:

PEREF began as a high-profile initiative aimed at bridging gaps within Saudi Arabia's tourism and cultural ambitions in event-relevant initiatives, sectors seen as critical for tourism, culture, and economic diversification. Initially conceptualized as a real estate-focused fund, PEREF was placed under the umbrella of the central holding company "CHC." The CHC itself was a new and developing entity. This positioning led to initial confusion, as the CHC was structured primarily for holding lending subsidiaries rather than operational oversight or direct investment. The CHC strategy was not yet ready or developed to facilitate the operation of existing companies or funds under its umbrella.

Stakeholders included high-level individuals (with experience in culture, tourism, and finance) appointed based on their roles with yet-to-be-developed definitions or responsibilities regarding the contribution to PEREF, adding complexity and opacity to the governance structure.

Diagnosis (Assessing the Challenges):

Despite being a startup rather than a traditional turnaround scenario, PEREF faced challenges strikingly similar to those of a distressed entity: ambiguous governance, uncertain financial structures, unrealistic funding assumptions, and stakeholder misalignment.

The most prominent challenge was PEREF's reliance on projected returns from products and services managed by another entity. Initial projections submitted to the PEREF board by those other entities indicated substantial revenue inflows. However, actual returns were alarmingly lower (only about 10-20 percent of forecasted amounts), resulting in budget shortfalls and funding instability.

Financially, PEREF was exposed due to limited oversight of funding sources. Operationally, ambiguity over stakeholder roles created friction and slowed decision-making. Strategically, PEREF faced challenges due to its initial ambiguous mission and unclear investment prioritization.

Turnaround Strategy Development (Startup Alignment with Turnaround Playbook):

Recognizing parallels to a turnaround, PEREF's leadership structured a robust strategy around core principles that can be found in the turnaround playbook:

- **Governance Restructuring:** This created clear board committees with defined mandates. Each board committee was established to include various stakeholders. At a project level, committees were designed to bring in involved entities from a range of stakeholders, minimizing overlaps and helping develop buy-in.
- **Financial Sustainability Initiatives:** Redesigned PEREF's funding strategy, shifting reliance from volatile projected revenues from unlinked entities toward stable financing sources, including strategic partnerships with prominent private-sector entities and bank financing arrangements totaling over SAR 7 billion.
- **Operational Prioritization:** Implemented rigorous capital allocation frameworks, prioritized key investment areas, and defined transparent criteria for project selection and approval.
- **Cultural Alignment and Talent Acquisition:** Emphasized attracting experienced professionals with experience in developing or investing in similar assets, establishing strong leadership, and embedding a culture of accountability, transparency, and excellence.

Internal conflicts arose primarily from territorial stakeholders. Managing these stakeholders required deliberate and diplomatic alignment strategies, including regular committee meetings, transparent communication, and collective stakeholder workshops, which facilitated mutual understanding and cooperation.

Implementation (Playbook in Action):

PEREF's implementation mirrored key phases of a turnaround:

1. **Securing Alternative Funding Sources:** Established partnerships with the private sector and secured bank term sheets, reducing the immediate pressure of uncertain revenue from Saudi Seasons.
2. **Governance and Operational Transparency:** Set up structured internal committees with clearly defined roles, responsibilities, and accountability, which enhances decision-making clarity.
3. **Capital Efficiency and Strategic Partnerships:** Optimize capital use by partnering strategically with private sector firms that have deep sector expertise and a vested interest in the operation, rather than just holding operational contracts or being silent investors.
4. **Culture and Talent Management:** Built a skilled team of 85 staff, with staff turnover below 5 percent annually, ensuring operational continuity and a performance-driven culture. Conducted regular town halls and provided anonymous feedback channels to encourage employee participation and innovation.

Key breakthroughs included successful bank financing, joint committees with stakeholders, robust internal processes documented extensively to sustain long-term excellence, and zero-comment external audit reports for three consecutive years.

Sustainability and Growth (Embedding Success):

To sustain the initial turnaround-like momentum, PEREF institutionalized stringent monitoring systems:

- **Cross-functional KPIs:** Established clear performance measures and shared accountability across departments, driving collaboration and transparency, ensuring that C-level performance is partially linked not just to department-level KPIs and staff satisfaction but also to overall company KPIs and collaboration KPIs.

- **Regular Monitoring:** Performed frequent weekly and monthly performance reviews and budget monitoring to address deviations immediately and preempt any potential issues.
- **Premortem Risk Analyses:** Conducted proactive risk assessments for priority assets and projects, anticipating and mitigating risks effectively.

PEREF's structured governance, rigorous financial controls, and cultural emphasis on accountability secured its continued success and operational integrity.

Outcomes (Measuring PEREF's Success):

PEREF successfully moved from concept to full operation in less than eighteen months:

- **Financial:** Secured over SAR 7 billion in bank financing and over two billion in private sector partnerships, significantly reducing dependency on volatile revenue sources
- **Operational:** Successfully executed investments and partnerships with three major private-sector local and global players, demonstrating private-sector confidence and validating PEREF's strategic direction and confidence in management in an environment where there are many opportunities for the private sector to choose from
- **Organizational:** Achieved high employee satisfaction, reflected in less than 5 percent annual turnover rates, underscoring a successful cultural and organizational structure
- **Strategic:** Implemented a rigorous governance framework, positioning PEREF for sustainable long-term growth beyond the initial launch phases

The application of turnaround principles, even in a startup context, enabled PEREF to quickly adapt, build resilience, and secure long-term strategic alignment and sustainability.

Key Lessons and Insights:

- **Turnaround Playbook Application in Startups:** PEREF's experience demonstrates that turnaround principles are highly effective for startups, particularly in scenarios involving complex stakeholder dynamics, ambiguous governance, and unstable financial assumptions.
- **Governance is Critical:** Clearly defined roles, responsibilities, and transparency significantly impact operational effectiveness and stakeholder alignment.
- **Proactive Financial Discipline:** Establishing alternative, reliable funding sources and disciplined financial management practices early on ensures resilience against volatile financial projections and uncertainties.
- **Talent and Culture Drive Results:** Investing in high-quality talent, precise performance metrics, and cultural cohesion directly impacts operational effectiveness and long-term sustainability.

CASE STUDY 2: AG&P—EXECUTING A STRATEGIC AND OPERATIONAL TURNAROUND

Initial Context:

AGP is a 125-year-old company established in the Philippines by American businesspeople to support local infrastructure projects.

Historically reliant on government subsidies, the company operated with heavy overhead, inefficiencies, and aging infrastructure. Its core business was fabrication-focused rather than offering full EPC (Engineering, Procurement, and Construction) solutions, limiting its value proposition and profitability potential. The organization was burdened by an extensive workforce and lacked structured governance, as well as clearly defined operational processes and strategic direction.

It had gone through multiple economic cycles and was hit particularly hard during the 2008 financial crisis; new business had completely dried up, and the parent company (DMCI) had lost interest in keeping it afloat.

Its customers were predominantly oil and gas companies in Asia, while competitors included more integrated EPC contractors offering comprehensive turnkey solutions, higher efficiency, and shorter project timelines.

Diagnosis:

Recognizing an opportunity for significant value creation, a private equity consortium acquired AG&P, identifying considerable upside from operational improvement, financial restructuring, and strategic repositioning. A thorough diagnosis revealed multiple challenges:

- **Operational Inefficiencies:** Long project timelines (over two years), cumbersome procurement processes, and inefficient use of labor and materials
- **Financial Dependency:** Heavy reliance on government subsidies and financial support rather than self-sustaining profitability
- **Weak Governance & Accountability:** Absence of credible decision-making authority, accountability frameworks, or transparent reporting mechanisms

- **Limited Strategic Capability:** Limited in-house design, engineering, and procurement capabilities significantly reduced competitiveness

The diagnostic stage highlighted the urgent need for comprehensive strategic and operational restructuring.

Investment Catalysts:

AGP's Fabrication Yard Location: The location, an hour south of Manila—with direct access to the deep sea—made it ideal for large-scale infrastructure overseas projects.

Trained Workforce: Although highly underutilized, it was apparent that AGP had a highly trained workforce. With a highly respected training institute, it could quickly ramp up its headcount.

Inexpensive Labor: The Philippine workforce was less costly than other large yards in the region (Korea, Taiwan, Japan, etc.). Chinese yards were suffering from poor quality and significant language issues.

Valuation: AGP was valued as a real estate asset with no value assigned to its assets or intellectual base.

Turnaround Strategy Development:

Leveraging the turnaround playbook methodology, we centered the strategy on four pillars:

- **Cost and Operational Restructuring:** Aggressive cost reductions, operational efficiencies (lean manufacturing, improved procurement processes), and infrastructure modernization
- **Strategic Pivot to EPC:** Transforming AG&P from a basic fabricator into a fully integrated EPC contractor offering design, procurement, and manpower solutions to reduce project timelines and increase value for customers
- **Governance Overhaul:** Implementing structured governance, clearer roles and responsibilities, executive accountability, and robust reporting frameworks

- **Culture and Workforce Transformation:** Addressing resistance and inertia through structured communication, workforce re-skilling, performance-based incentives, and clearly defined career growth pathways

Stakeholder buy-in was secured through a comprehensive communication strategy that emphasized mutual benefits, sustainability, and positive impacts on employee welfare and regional economic growth.

Implementation:

The turnaround was executed methodically, aligned precisely with the playbook phases and philosophy:

- **New leadership**: It was evident that AGP was suffering from a lack of vision and a cohesive strategy. Before implementing a new business plan, it was integral to infuse new leadership with long-term performance-linked compensation that included an interesting *clawback feature* to ensure managers' interests aligned with those of the shareholders.
- **Governance and Leadership:** This should entail the immediate appointment of a new CEO, an experienced leader in the field with a strong alignment, as he has invested in the company during its acquisition. Additionally, an entirely new board of directors and fresh C-suite executives should be appointed.
- **Operational Restructuring:**

With the help of technology, we focused on disintermediating and creating a vertically integrated framework. Design, Engineering, Procurement, Construction/Fabrication, Commissioning, Manpower, and Operational Maintenance capabilities were all available under one roof.

Such a comprehensive exercise in streamlining a wide range of services allowed us to remove multiple middlemen (intermediaries) and reduce overheads and competitive pricing.

- **Operational Excellence:** Implemented lean manufacturing practices, integrated digital procurement solutions, and enhanced

project management processes, reducing refinery construction timelines from two years to approximately nine months, doubling capacity.
- **Financial Stabilization:** As part of our turnaround plan, we raised substantial capital to support the business's short-term goals. This included providing necessary working capital to support bidding for specific projects where AGP was competitive.

Once the business had achieved sustenance, we institutionalized financial discipline with comprehensive monthly, quarterly, and annual reviews. Fortunately, AGP had minimum loan obligations, so we could establish credit lines with the banks to support ongoing operations. We also negotiated competitive terms for a long-term loan facility in case AGP can bid and win large-scale projects.

Strategic Refocusing:

With financial resources on hand and operational restructuring in place, we could reposition the company toward MODULARIZATION, where large-scale structures were built or assembled from several smaller modules, similar to how a LEGO® set is constructed. This allowed us to compete for projects in faraway areas where modular construction was much more economical (as opposed to on-site stick-built structures).

The timeline compressed significantly, and overall build quality improved drastically, as nearly all fabrication was conducted in a controlled environment, such as a yard or factory. Once fabrication and testing were completed in our yard, the modules were shipped to their final destination for on-site assembly.

Most of the yards with modular capability were located in developed countries and had significantly higher costs. Therefore, we were easily able to compete and win some significant projects.

Cultural and Workforce Engagement

- Introduced structured incentive programs, intensive training and re-skilling, continuous dialogue, and a culture focused on quality, efficiency, and customer value.

- Minimum use of external consultants in AG&P, except in providing expertise in strategy formulation, cultural transformation, corporate tax advice, and change management.

Sustainability and Growth:

Post-turnaround sustainability hinged on structured governance, robust performance management, and continuous innovation. AG&P institutionalized:

- **Long-term client contracts** are tied explicitly to performance efficiency, quality metrics, and delivery timelines.
- **Continuous innovation** occurred through internal Centers of Excellence (CoEs) and regular process audits.
- **Employee engagement and retention programs** ensured a continued high-performance culture, commitment, and morale.
- **Strategic partnerships**, particularly with private equity investors, facilitated expansion into new geographical markets (Europe and North America) and product offerings.

AG&P became sustainably competitive by consistently reinvesting cost savings into innovation, technology upgrades, and market expansion initiatives.

Luck Favors the Brave!!!

While we were competing for modular construction projects, India opened up its City Gas Distribution (CGD) market to internal and external private competition.

With extensive expertise in steel fabrication, we decided to bid aggressively for various concessions. With some clever pricing strategies, we outbid Adani Enterprises to win eleven sizeable concessions covering a population of about 110 million people.

Once we started working on a few concessions, Think Gas (a subsidiary of I Square Capital with six concessions) approached us for a possible merger. After some interesting negotiations and a fresh capital infusion from Osaka Gas, JBIC, and JOIN, we successfully consummated a merger that resulted in one of India's most prominent City Gas Distribution players.

Eventual Exit:

The valuation of this joint entity was circa $1.8 billion in the last round (2023) and is expected to approach circa $3 billion as we plan a public market exit in late 2026. Thus, what started as an insignificant investment (~$37 million) has resulted in an eventual valuation of circa $355 million with still more upside from the upcoming IPO.

Outcomes:

The turnaround was a demonstrable success with substantial value creation and business sustainability:

- **Financial:** Transformed a modest initial investment (~USD 32 million) into an enterprise value exceeding ~USD 1.8 billion, positioning AG&P as a highly valuable global player worth around USD 3 billion in the coming days
- **Operational:** Drastically reduced project timelines from two years to approximately nine months, significantly increasing operational efficiency, capacity, zero accidents, and market share
- **Organizational:** Achieved a cultural transformation, increased employee satisfaction, significantly improved retention, and built a performance-driven environment focused on continuous improvement
- **Strategic:** Successfully transitioned from an assembly-based fabricator into a fully integrated EPC solutions provider with a robust global market presence and major global Blue-Chip Clients

Key Lessons and Insights:

- **Leadership and Governance are Crucial:** Swift executive and board-level changes immediately catalyzed turnaround momentum and provided a carefully selected and proper incentive to the C-level.

- **Integration Drives Competitiveness:** Transitioning from assembly to fully integrated EPC provided sustainable competitive advantages and significantly higher profitability.
- **Cultural Transformation Underpins Success:** Engaging employees, providing incentives, and demonstrating the personal benefits of operational and strategic changes significantly reduced resistance to new ownership, especially when transitioning from a government-owned company to a private one.
- **Private Equity Partnership Adds Strategic Value:** PE investors brought capital, strategic guidance, and market expansion opportunities, significantly enhancing enterprise value and fostering future confidence in further funding rounds.

CASE STUDY 3—DUET INTERNATIONAL HOTELS (DIH), INDIA

Background:

Duet International Hotels (DIH) was established in 2007 by a UK-based asset manager to benefit from the growing middle class in India, where business travel was increasing but business hotels were in short supply.

Most of the assets were bought during the peak reached before the 2008 financial crisis, and DIH paid a hefty premium for most of them. The hotel industry was hit severely during and after the crisis, with daily room rates dropping by 50 to 70 percent.

Diagnosis:

DIH was a subscale operator of six business hotels that IHC managed under the relatively unknown "Holiday Inn Express" brand, which was new to India at the time. Its business model, which offered minimum amenities such as breakfast, was against the local culture and norms.

During India's 2005–2007 economic boom, many landowners decided to become hotel operators, resulting in an oversupply of fresh properties and rooms that overwhelmed demand. Nearly all the hotels were forced into a price war to cover fixed costs, especially the high-interest expense.

Context:

DIH management kept the company afloat, but by early 2016, it was obvious that interest costs alone were higher than the EBITDA, and long-term prospects were quite bleak.

As Duet sought outside investors, KKR conducted detailed operational, financial, and legal diligence and offered a highly punitive term sheet. Asiya Investments was a minority investor in DIH and exercised its first right of refusal by extending the same terms as KKR, which the Duet board accepted.

Investment Thesis:

We understood that most newcomers in this market were also small-scale with no financial cushion. Hence, if we could withstand short-term financial pressure in this battle of the fittest, it would reduce competition over the medium to long term.

It was well understood that in a growing economy where GDP growth consistently approached eight to ten percent, *incremental demand for business travel, therefore, for business hotels, would be strong and consistent.*

Turnaround Strategy

In our short-term plan, we aggressively pursued rebranding the hotels to "Fairfield/Four Points by Marriott," which is the largest brand in India and globally. Such rebranding was very well received, and Marriott was keen to extend us an olive branch to kickstart its presence in the "Business Hotels" space.

In addition, we hired a seasoned team of hospitality veterans to manage the properties, which provided us with significant flexibility in pricing and enabled us to offer upscale amenities to the guests.

Based on extensive turnaround experience, we implemented a transparent governance structure that recognized and rewarded outperformance. All these managers were awarded options and restricted stock to align with their strategic interests.

We encouraged *"out-of-the-box thinking"* to all our employees, which resulted in an enhanced guest experience. These guests consistently *ranked our properties at the highest level in our category.*

Our approach to offering rebates to online travel agents (OTA) was well received. We were pushed up in the marketing plans of these OTAs, thus increasing our overall occupancy rates.

From Bad to Worse:

With the start of COVID-19, all the hotels in India shut down. While other owners were panicking and abandoning hospitality assets, we worked aggressively on refinancing. With minimal equity capital infusion, we convinced the banks to significantly lower interest rates and provide extensive moratoriums (interest: 2 years, principal: 5 years).

Although the supply of new properties and rooms had already slowed before the COVID pandemic, it entered negative territory, with many existing facilities converting into residential units.

Silver Lining:

As the COVID-19 shock abated and business travel resumed, supply could not keep up with the "revenge" travel demand, resulting in significant pricing power. Our room rates almost tripled, and even then, occupancies were very high (about 90 percent). We moved these properties from lower corporate rates to OTA, which are generally approximately 30 to 50 percent higher.

Strive for Scale:

With the properties generating record profits, we reached out to multiple other hoteliers in pursuit of scale. We had to ensure that any suitor had a *strategic alignment* and could provide the necessary synergies in any merger.

Finally, we merged with SAMHI Enterprises, resulting in a combined entity with nearly 10,000 rooms and a diverse portfolio of strategically located hotels. It was a merger that benefited both parties through the scale and immense operational synergies.

Eventual Exit:

With significant scale and record profitability, it was agreed that the combined entity was ready for an IPO in the local Indian market.

The company was finally listed on the Indian stock exchange in 2023, garnering significant interest from both local and international investors. Over five transformative years, we not only salvaged our original investment—which was on track to be lost under KKR's control—but also delivered a threefold *return on newly infused capital*. It is a classic case of patience and perseverance supported by a sound investment thesis that eventually resulted in a meaningful turnaround and highly lucrative returns.

Appendix

A.1 Key Turnaround Benchmarks and Metrics

Purpose: Provide quantitative targets and industry norms to help turnaround teams gauge performance gaps and set realistic improvement goals.

Metric	Typical Pre-Turnaround Values	Turnaround Target Range	Notes/References
Liquidity Ratio (Current)	0.8–1.1	1.2–1.5+	Many successful turnarounds aim for a current ratio >1.2
DSO (Days Sales Outstanding)	60–90 days	30–45 days	(BCG, *Cash Excellence*, 2020)
Net Debt/EBITDA	4.0–6.0x	2.0–3.0x	Reducing leverage is critical for lender confidence
EBITDA Margin Improvement	-2% to 5% (pre-turnaround)	+5–10pp margin uplift	(McKinsey, *Transformation at Scale*, 2019)
SG&A as % of Revenue	20–25%	15–18%	(KPMG, *Cost Optimization Study*, 2021)
Inventory Turnover	4–6 turns	8–12 turns	Lean inventory can free substantial working capital

A.2 Manufacturing-Specific Benchmarks

Metric	Typical Pre-Turnaround	Turnaround Target	Notes
OEE (Overall Equipment Effectiveness)	50–65%	75–85%+	Lean & Six Sigma improvements often yield 15–20% OEE increases.
Scrap/Defect Rate	3–5% of production	<2%	Tighter QC and root-cause analysis reduce scrap significantly.
Capacity Utilization	60–70%	80–90%	Footprint consolidation or demand alignment can drive synergy.
Lead Time (Days)	10–15 days	5–8 days	Shorter lead times boost customer satisfaction.

A.3 Services-Specific Benchmarks

Metric	Typical Pre-Turnaround	Turnaround Target	Notes
Customer Churn Rate	15–20% annually	<10%	Enhanced service quality & loyalty programs key for retention.
Revenue per Employee (RPE)	Low or stagnant	+15–30% improvement	Automation & improved processes raise productivity.
Average Resolution Time (Support)	48–72 hours	12–24 hours	Digital tools (chatbots, RPA) accelerate resolution.
Customer Satisfaction (NPS)	<30 (on a -100 to 100 scale)	50+	(McKinsey, *NPS as a Growth Indicator*, 2018)

B. Sample Case Studies/Real-World Scenarios

Purpose: Demonstrate how the frameworks and actions described in the playbook can translate into measurable results.

B.1 Manufacturing Turnaround Case

Context: A mid-sized automotive components manufacturer faced high overhead, excess inventory, and poor on-time delivery performance.

Immediate Actions (Phase 1 and Rapid Stabilization):

- Implemented a thirteen-week cash flow forecast
- Froze discretionary spending, renegotiated major supplier contracts, and liquidated slow-moving inventory.

Key Interventions (Phases 2 and 3):

- Adopted Lean Six Sigma to reduce scrap from 4 percent to 1.5 percent
- Consolidated from 3 plants to 2, raising capacity utilization from 65 percent to 85 percent
- Revamped sales strategy, focusing on higher-margin product lines

Outcomes (Phase 4 and Sustainability):

- Improved EBITDA margin from 4 percent to 12 percent within 12 months
- Freed up ~$15 million in working capital via inventory and payables optimization
- Built an in-house "continuous improvement office" to sustain gains

Reference: BCG Whitepaper, Automotive Turnarounds in Emerging Markets (2020)

B.2 Service Industry Turnaround Case

Context: A regional healthcare services provider suffered from high staff turnover, negative cash flow, and low patient satisfaction ratings.

Immediate Actions:

- Rapid triage of accounts receivable to improve cash flow.
- Introduced telehealth pilots for quick expansions in underserved geographies.
- Key Interventions:
- Centralized HR processes and introduced performance-based incentives. Turnover fell from 22 percent to 14 percent in 6 months.
- Automated administrative tasks (billing, scheduling) using RPA. Cut overhead costs by 15 percent.

Appendix   145

Outcomes:

- Patient satisfaction (NPS) increased from 28 to 55 in a year.
- A cost savings of approximately $8 million was achieved and reinvested into a new telemedicine platform.
- Negotiated favorable insurer contracts, improving revenue predictability.

Reference: McKinsey & Company, Healthcare 2.0: Restructuring for Patient-Centric Services (2019)

C. Industry-Specific Best Practices

C.1 Manufacturing

Total Productive Maintenance (TPM):

- Aim to reduce unplanned downtime by 30–50 percent (KPMG, Industrial Ops Report, 2021).
- Use predictive analytics (IoT sensors) to schedule proactive maintenance.

Footprint Optimization and Consolidation:

- Evaluate factory locations versus demand centers.
- Divest or repurpose underutilized assets to free capital.

Quality Systems and Certifications:

- Achieve ISO/TS standards if relevant and open new revenue channels.

C.2 Services

Service Portfolio Rationalization:

- Identify unprofitable service lines or packages.
- Standardize offerings to simplify training and reduce errors.

Customer Experience Transformation:

- Introduce real-time dashboards (AI-based) to monitor satisfaction.
- Automate front-end tasks using chatbots or self-service portals.

Human Capital Strategy:

- Upskill the workforce to reduce reliance on manual tasks.
- Implement flexible scheduling or telecommuting to minimize overhead.

C.3 Retail and Consumer

Omnichannel Integration:

- Align e-commerce, mobile apps, and brick-and-mortar for a consistent customer experience.

Inventory and Merchandising Optimization:

- Use advanced analytics to forecast demand.
- Minimize stock-outs and markdowns.

C.4 Energy and Utilities

Commodity Price Hedging:

- Adopt risk management frameworks to hedge volatile inputs or outputs (EY, 2020).

Asset Portfolio Review:

- Divest older, inefficient assets or enter joint ventures for infrastructure upgrades.

D. Additional Frameworks and Tools

Kotter's 8-Step Change Model:

- Create Urgency
- Build Coalitions
- Form Vision
- Communicate
- Remove Barriers
- Short-Term Wins
- Build on Change
- Anchor in Culture

McKinsey 7S:

- Strategy
- Structure
- Systems
- Skills
- Style
- Staff
- Shared Values

Evaluate alignment and synergy across these seven dimensions.

Porter's Value Chain:

Identify key high-value activities (inbound logistics, operations, outbound logistics, marketing, service) to reduce costs or differentiate.

BCG Growth-Share Matrix:

It helps categorize product lines or business units as Stars, Cash Cows, Dogs, or Question Marks, and is helpful in portfolio rationalization.

Balanced Scorecard:

Ensures performance metrics extend beyond finances to customer perspective, internal processes, learning, and growth.

E. Communication and Governance Templates

Stakeholder Communication Matrix:

Columns

Stakeholder Group | Key Interests | Message Focus | Frequency | Channels | Owner

For example, lenders require weekly short-term liquidity updates, while employees look for monthly reassurance about job security.

Steering Committee or Turnaround Office Charter

Purpose: Oversee day-to-day execution, hold weekly progress reviews, and maintain risk registers.

Membership: CRO/Interim Manager, CFO, department heads, PMO lead

Milestone and RACI (Responsible, Accountable, Consulted, Informed) Table

Purpose: Ensure clarity of roles for each primary deliverable (debt restructuring, cost reduction, capacity rationalization, etc.). For example, the CFO is accountable for weekly liquidity updates. The CRO is responsible for implementing cost-cutting measures and other initiatives aimed at reducing expenses.

F. References and Recommended Reading

BCG:

Effective Turnarounds: Funding the Journey, 2020.

Manufacturing Turnarounds in Emerging Markets, 2020.

McKinsey & Company:

Changing Change Management, 2019.

Healthcare 2.0: Restructuring for Patient-Centric Services, 2019.

KPMG:

Appendix

Cost Optimization Study, 2021.

Cash Preservation in Turnarounds, 2021.

EY:

Robotic Process Automation in Services, 2020.

John Kotter: Leading Change, 1996.